POINTS NORTH

**Discover Hidden Campgrounds, Natural Wonders,
and Waterways of the Upper Peninsula**

Mikel B. Classen

ModernHistoryPress
Ann Arbor, MI

Library of Congress Cataloging-in-Publication Data

Names: Classen, Mikel B., author.
Title: Points North : discover hidden campgrounds, natural wonders, and
waterways of the Upper Peninsula / Mikel B. Classen.
Other titles: Discover hidden campgrounds, natural wonders, and waterways
of the Upper Peninsula
Description: Ann Arbor, MI : Modern History Press, [2020] | Includes
bibliographical references and index. | Summary: "In this book, the
author has listed 40 destinations from every corner of Michigan's Upper
Peninsula that have places of interest. Some reflect rich history, while
others highlight natural wonders that abound across the peninsula."--
Provided by publisher.
Identifiers: LCCN 2019043639 (print) | LCCN 2019043640 (ebook) | ISBN
9781615994908 (paperback) | ISBN 9781615994915 (hardcover) | ISBN
9781615994922 (kindle edition) | ISBN 9781615994922 (epub)
Subjects: LCSH: Camp sites, facilities, etc.--Michigan--Upper Peninsula. |
Trails--Michigan--Upper Peninsula. | Parks--Michigan--Upper Peninsula. |
Outdoor recreation--Michigan--Upper Peninsula--Guidebooks.
Classification: LCC GV54.M5 C53 2020 (print) | LCC GV54.M5 (ebook) | DDC
917.74/9068--dc23
LC record available at https://lccn.loc.gov/2019043639
LC ebook record available at https://lccn.loc.gov/2019043640

ISBN-13 978-1-61599-490-8 paperback
ISBN-13 978-1-61599-491-5 hardcover
ISBN-13 978-1-61599-492-2 eBook
Cataloging-in-Publication data is available at the Library of Congress online site

Learn about the author's other books at www.MikelClassen.com and unlock extra content for this book
at www.PointsNorthBooks.com/sites

Distributed by Ingram (USA/CAN/AU), Bertram's Books (UK/EU)

Published by
Modern History Press
5145 Pontiac Trail
Ann Arbor, MI 48105

www.ModernHistoryPress.com
info@ModernHistoryPress.com
Tollfree 888-761-6268
Fax 734-663-6861

CONTENTS

Dedication

This book is dedicated to the Upper Peninsula of Michigan. Its extraordinary beauty has touched my soul every day, and I hope that some of that is reflected in this book. I also want to dedicate this book to Mary Lina Underwood, my wife, without whose wholehearted support this book wouldn't have been written.

Introduction

This book has been a labor of love that spans many years. The love is for Michigan's Upper Peninsula (U.P.), its places and people. I've spent many years exploring the wilderness of the U.P., and one thing has become apparent. No matter what part you find yourself in, fascinating sights are around every corner. There are parks, wilderness areas, and museums. There are ghost towns and places named after legends. There are trails to be walked and waterways to be paddled. In the U.P., life is meant to be lived to the fullest.

Many years ago, I started writing a feature column called "Off the Beaten Path." The idea was, for every column, to check out a new place that wasn't your usual destination, such as Tahquamenon Falls and Mackinac Island. Thus began a lifetime of discovery. The column did well.

One day, my editor received a call from *Reader's Digest Books* wanting permission to use the name "Off the Beaten Path." She gave it. I was horrified. Now we could no longer use the column name I had established for several years. I settled on "Points North," which I have used since, and it now graces the cover of this book.

One can't write a book like this without noticing changes to some of the destinations originally slated for inclusion. Specifically, they had disap-

peared. Most were parks with campgrounds that no longer exist—ghost parks. I come across more and more every day.

Across the Upper Peninsula are dozens of state parks, state forest campgrounds, and U.S. Forest Service campgrounds. Many are in remote places that typically have fewer than 10 campsites. One can have a solitary experience at such locations, as, oftentimes, the number of campers is zero to five. In other words, the campsites' remoteness makes them rarely used, and therein lies the problem. As budgets are cut, these low-use sites are always in danger of elimination. We need people to find, use, and enjoy these places, because they are slowly going away. Some of these places are highlighted in the book, but many more exist. Chippewa County alone has over 30 of these remote-adventure opportunities.

In this book, I've listed 40 destinations from every corner of the U.P. that have places of interest. Some reflect rich history, while others highlight natural wonders that abound across the peninsula. So many sights exist, in fact, that after a lifetime of exploration, I'm still discovering new and fascinating places that I've never seen or heard of. So, join in the adventures. The Upper Peninsula is an open book—the one that's in your hand.

Mikel B. Classen, 2019

Au Sable Point Lighthouse Alger County

Au Sable Point Lighthouse as it appears today. Its light still shines across Lake Superior.

Pictured Rocks National Lakeshore, located on the North Coast of Michigan's Upper Peninsula, is well known for its scenic beauty, but visitors to the park often overlook its one man-made attraction. Most visitors drive by the nearly unmarked Au Sable Point Lighthouse without ever realizing that the fully intact, historically significant, still functioning lighthouse is there.

Located at the scene of several shipwrecks, this graphic example of life along Lake Superior's shipwreck coast is located 12 miles west of Grand Marais. The remains of the *Mary Jarecki, Sitka,* and *Gale Staples* can still be seen along the shore. Even now, Au Sable Point Light stands isolated on a battered spit of sandstone that endures the fiercest wrath Superior can muster. To the east stands the majesty of Grand Sable Dunes. To the west, forest and miles of beach that merge into the cliffs of Pictured Rocks. Continuing six feet under the surface of the lake, the point becomes a mile-long sandstone reef, a dangerous trap for sailors.

It must have been terrifying, sailing hard toward Grand Marais, a harbor of refuge, the screaming winds and the massive waves pounding against the ship, and then the sickening crunch as the Au Sable sandstone destroyed the hull. Plunging into the angry ice-cold surf would be the only option for survival. Then it was in god's hands.

In 1871, according to the *Marquette Mining Journal*, it was deemed that "in all navigation of Lake Superior, there is none more dreaded by the mariner than that from Whitefish Point to Grand Island." Further, a light was thought more a necessity at Au Sable Point than at any other unprotected location in the district.

Consequently, a light was constructed there and went into operation in August 1874. The same light still stands over 125 years later, a monument to a bygone era.

The light tower is 85 feet high, and the base of it extends 23 feet underground. Written accounts describe when the wind blew so hard that light keepers feared the lighthouse would topple because the tower shook so much. Picture it: You're tending the light in the top of the tower when the winds of Superior shake and batter everything around. The fear grows in your belly that it all can come down around you.

Walking about the property, one can easily envision the harshness of life that must have permeated even the most mundane of daily chores. Isolation and loneliness were constant companions, and those who couldn't handle it didn't last long. Originally it was planned that only one keeper would run the light, but within a year an assistant was assigned, and then a third was put on. But even then the isolation was nearly unbearable. One lighthouse keeper wrote that Au Sable "was just as isolated as if it were 30 miles from land."

When the lighthouse was first built, there were no roads (the first access road was built in 1939). The only access to Au Sable Point (originally called Big Sable Point) was by boat, usually from Grand Marais, though boats came from Munising as well. Most years the residents were isolated for six months without seeing another soul.

The buildings of the main complex included the main lighthouse keeper's building, the assistant's building with the light tower, the fog-signal building, the boathouse, and the oil houses.

Of course, one could stave off the boredom a bit with daily routines. Keeping the steam up in the fog signal and oil filled in the lighthouse were full-time jobs. They were also necessary jobs—a shipwreck on Lake Superior meant death. The lighthouse keeper's dedication to routine saved lives. Quiet and no emergencies meant the keeper did the job.

When a wreck did happen (after the lighthouse was built the instances dropped), the keepers had to battle the deadliest waters to save sailors' lives. They used boats a fraction of the size of the ships that the angry waters had just destroyed. A very special individual was needed to deal with life at Au Sable Point.

Au Sable Point is located 1.5 miles northeast of the lower Hurricane River Campground in Pictured Rocks National Lakeshore. The Hurricane River Campground is 12 miles west of Grand Marais on County Road H-58. Visitors park their vehicles in the day-use area and then hike out to the lighthouse along the North Country Trail. Walking the shoreline off the trail will lead to remnants of shipwrecks, the old ribs leaving an eerie feeling of disasters past.

The Au Sable Lighthouse complex has been fully restored, with the last build-

A kayaker paddles past the shipwreck of the Gale Staples which lies on the shore near the point. (top)
Historical picture of Au Sable Lighthouse in 1874 when it was built. (left)
Author standing atop some of the wreckage of the Mary Jarecki. (middle)
The walkway from the fog building to the keeper's quarters. (right)

ing finished in 2002. A new visitor's center and bookstore will open in what used to be the main lighthouse keeper's building. Interpretive programs run daily during the summer months, along with lighthouse tours. On your next trip to the Pictured Rocks National Lakeshore area, don't miss the point. Nowhere will you have the opportunity for a Lake Superior experience like this.

One of the best ways to enjoy Au Sable Point is to camp there. On the North Country Trail, about a short half mile past the lighthouse complex, are several tent sites for camping. The view here is breathtaking, and the sites are well sheltered. This way to spend quality time on the shore of Lake Superior is my personal favorite.

If you don't want to get quite so remote, the Hurricane River Campground is also a wonderful place to camp. It has a lovely beach, and the Hurricane River supports excellent fishing.

For more information on the Au Sable Point Lighthouse, contact Pictured Rocks National Lakeshore at 906-387-3700 or check out its website at www.nps.gov/piro or via http://pointsnorth-books.com/sites

Au Train Rising
Alger County

The village of Au Train as seen from M-28.

Across the Upper Peninsula are many small communities; most struggle daily to survive. Some don't succeed and become historical footnotes. Au Train is one of those small towns—or so it seemed a few years ago. In recent years, the town has been on the rise.

For a century, Au Train has depended on its natural beauty for its lifeblood. Au Train Lake, Au Train River, and the sand beaches of Au Train Bay on Lake Superior made for a powerful lure in the early 1900s. As resorts sprang up, the one-time logging town became a tourist destination. It has remained so to this day, but in the late '90s and early 2000s, the community seemed on its last legs. Resorts were for sale, and the few businesses that remained either barely eked out a living or failed completely.

Suddenly Au Train is transforming—not away from the nice, small town it always has been but into a recreational destination once again. As one shop keeper put it, "When kayaking became popular in Munising and Pictured Rocks, they found us too."

The Au Train River, similar to paddling the Au Sable of the Lower Peninsula, has always been the best river in the U.P. for a canoe or kayak. Even pontoons cruise it periodically. Not only is it fairly large and wide, but also it connects Au Train Lake with Lake Superior. The river meanders a lot. When it leaves Au Train Lake, the river flows under Forest Lake Road. It then meanders for several miles before going under

Forest Lake Road again, not even a mile from where it crossed before. Then it flows for a few more miles into Lake Superior, again barely a mile from where it crossed before. It doesn't get more paddle-friendly than that. You can take the river in pieces, or you can start at the Au Train Lake Campground and paddle all of Au Train Lake and River.

Au Train Lake Campground is a U.S. Forest Service campground and is located on the south end of Au Train Lake. This 32-site campground is primitive—no hookups and vault bathrooms, though the bathrooms are well taken care of and nice. A boat launch for public access to Au Train Lake and the River is at the site. Like many U.S.F.S. campgrounds, no ATVs are allowed, though the area has an intricate ATV trail system and Au Train Township itself is quite ATV-friendly.

The Au Train Lake Campground also contains the Au Train Songbird Trail, developed by the Michigan Department of Natural Resources, U.S. Forest Service, Hiawatha National Forest, and lots of local folks. The 2-mile interpretive hiking trail through U.P. forest eventually follows an incredibly picturesque stream. Signs depict local songbirds and describe how to recognize them. Local stores sell a songbird cassette tape with each of the birdcalls that are meant to be played along the trail at the signs. You're on your own for a player.

Alger County is famous for its waterfalls, and Au Train has them too. The turnoff for Au Train Falls runs east, about 100 feet before M-94 when travelling south on Forest Lake Road. It is poorly marked but worth looking for. Au Train Falls consists of two falls: the lower falls, which is easier to access and therefore more visited, and the upper falls, which causes some to say "Am I crazy trying to get to these falls?" The

Forest scene

slope leading down to it is very steep and fit for mountain goats. Naturally, I had to investigate. South of the Upper Au Train Falls, the Au Train River is dammed, and the steel spillway runs across the upper falls past the lower for some of the area's hydroelectricity. This can make the upper falls seem not to flow well, whereas the lower falls flows hard. As I stood at the bottom of the upper falls, I saw no less than six small streams, all coming from springs in the surrounding rock, flowing hard, feeding the Au Train River. This small cradle of life, refusing to be beaten by logging and dams, still flowed, making the Au Train one of the clearest rivers in Michigan.

With cars lining the road at access points to the river, the town of Au Train seems to be prospering. The Northwoods Resort has set up shop at

Old cabin overlooking the picturesque Au Train River, a paddlers paradise. (top)

Where Au Train Lake and Au Train River meet. Some of the historical old resorts can be seen in the distance. (middle)

Au Train Falls in mid-summer. (bottom)

daily along the Au Train River! The food isn't bad either.

The food isn't bad anywhere in Au Train. The Au Train Grocery makes good meaty pasties daily. It also serves subs, but I couldn't get by the pasties. The A&L Party Store, the first place you see when you come into Au Train, serves an excellent pizza by any standards and oven-baked subs that were being made here in Au Train long before Quiznos and those other chains thought of it. When I met my wife many moons ago, she lived in Au Train, and we ate here on a regular basis. It's still as good, and it's still owned by the same family. Actually, the same person cooked my sub now as back then.

Au Train is one of the oldest place names along the Lake Superior coast. It was the site of Native American fishing and home of the legendary Face in the Rock carving. Then it became a fur trading post. When Schoolcraft County was reorganized to create Alger County, Au Train was the first county seat. It was home of one of the first UP newspapers, the *Au Train Alpha*. At one time, nearly one thousand people lived around Au Train. Some of the old homes of Au Train still reflect those early days. Where the railroad once ran, ATVs now follow the old route.

It seems fitting that a place of such antiquity should continue to rise up and thrive in spite of the odds of the modern world. Those that have lived in the Upper Peninsula know what it is. The Finns called it *sisu*. It's the refusal to quit when signs indicate you should. Whether Au Train found life or life found Au Train doesn't matter. What matters is Au Train is rising. How far or how long remains to be seen, but right now the odds are looking good. More info at http://pointsnorthbooks.com/sites

the river crossings, renting canoes and spotting paddlers to launch points along the river. The resort is even now renting fat-tire bikes. The amazing thing to me was the lunch truck it had set up along the river at one of the pull-out points. The truck is parked

Big Knob State Forest Campground and Hiking Area Mackinac County

Lake Michigan beach at Big Knob Campground. The sandy shore here is great for summer.

This little hidden gem is a few miles west of Naubinway off U.S. 2. Situated on the shore of Lake Michigan, the Big Knob State Forest Campground and Hiking Area is usually known by word of mouth. But, secrets have a way of revealing themselves. Deep in the heart of the Mackinac State Forest, surrounded by primordial forest, an extraordinary experience awaits for one who is willing to find it.

Big Knob is a quiet place and is meant to be that way. With three developed hiking paths, and no public access for boats, noise is a stranger here. But paddlers might want to take note. Carrying a kayak, paddleboard, or canoe to the shore is easy. The reward is a nice paddle on a portion of the Lake Michigan Water Trail.

A nice sand beach here seems to cradle the Lake Michigan waves and is perfect for swimming, paddling, or even a hike along the sand, as it isn't so soft that walking is difficult. This eases the task of transporting your craft as well. Transport wheels for kayaks work well, though only a couple hundred yards separate the shore from the parking lot.

The real attraction of this park is the hiking trails. The three trails each have their own appeal and degree of difficulty, though none are excessively difficult. Descriptions follow.

Marsh Lake (top)
Big Knob campsite (bottom)

Big Knob Crow Lake (top)
Marsh Lake Trail (bottom)

Marsh Lake Trail

The trailhead for Marsh Lake Trail is at the day- use parking lot at Big Knob, and the trail is an easy hike through the woods. It winds deep into a marshland that has wilderness beauty in a short walk. The trail, about 1.5 miles long, loops back to the road a few hundred yards from its starting point. One can find blueberries along the trail in late July. Marsh Lake itself is an extensive wetland that abounds with wildlife.

Crow Lake Trail

This trail begins about 2 miles up the entrance road to Big Knob and runs about 2.5 miles, requiring a medium-level hiking ability. Many ups and downs roll along the trail, but the effort is worth it. The heavy pine presence in the forest exudes a pleasant fragrance. Crow Lake itself is a wilderness lake, and the hike down to the shore is steep. Although the trail proceeds from that point, don't follow it. Turn around and head back. It is poorly marked and eventually becomes impossible to follow.

Big Knob Trail

This trailhead is also two miles up the entrance road, across from the Crow Lake trailhead. With a length of a half mile, Big Knob Trail is mostly uphill. The hiker catches glimpses of Big Knob Lake in the distance, but foliage blocks most views. Ideally the trail should be hiked when the leaves are off. The path through the trees is beautiful, and the ridge it follows gives the hike its own character.

The Big Knob State Forest Campground and recreation area has 40 sites. The campsites are primitive, and so are the facilities. The water pump is by hand. Large RVs have a difficult time maneuvering in the tight access roads. Sites are largely situated in a hardwood forest in a hollow near the shore, nicely sheltered from any Lake Michigan tantrums.

Big Knob is one of those overlooked places that simply shouldn't be. Its remote wilderness hiking trails give it a flavor that isn't matched other places. More info at or http://pointsnorthbooks.com/sites

Big Two Hearted River Luce County

I stepped into the stone-and-sand-bottom river with my waders on and fly rod in hand. My creel bounced against my side, making a hollow sound as I braced myself against the force of the current. From the start, I'd made the decision to do it exactly as he had in the story. I sort indulged a fantasy. "Big Two-Hearted River," one of Ernest Hemingway's finest short stories and one of the Nick Adams outdoors tales, is set here in Michigan's Upper Peninsula, with the river running north of Newberry. The story is about trout-fishing the river and is the epitome of outdoors writing. Hemingway spent a good amount of time fishing the area, and the story makes clear how truly wonderful trout fishing is and the near reverence afforded the sport by the avid trout man. When I read it, I thought taking an excursion up to the Two-Hearted River to see if all the luck Hemingway seemed to have was simply writer's license would be interesting. What I found was a lot more than just a good fishing hole.

No doubt, Hemingway would probably no longer recognize the area, but I'm sure he would still find it as enjoyable. Over the years, much of the area has been logged and some of it is still in the process of logging. Fur-

Misty morning

thermore, the area was hit hard a few years back by fire. Consequently, some tracts are completely clear, others have full growth, and every stage of development exists in between. Don't get me wrong—clear-cutting has proven to be not all bad, and I'll get into why later. The river and its bed remain unchanged, and the surrounding for-

Swing bridge walkway

est sports the old deep hard and soft wood mixture so wonderfully panoramic and so typical for the Upper Peninsula.

The mouth of the Two Hearted River is located 30 miles north of Newberry. Take M-123 north 17 miles to County Road 500. Then go north 6 miles to County Road 414. Take this west for 4 miles. You'll go by a place called Pike Lake. It's worth a stop for a look and maybe a swim or some fishing, and a campground and store are nearby. Continue to County Road 412, and go north 3 more miles. Here is a Michigan State Park Campground that consists of 45 primitive sites, without electrical or water/sewage hookups, costing only a few bucks a night. The campground can serve as the base for your activities.

The campground is situated right on the riverbank that has a long beautiful sandbar for a beach. The beach, rumored to be prime agate-hunting area, runs for hundreds of yards between the river and Lake Superior. Connecting the park to the beach is a suspension footbridge that sways in the wind, giving an eerie feeling—but it is exceptionally safe.

The bridge leads to a site of historical note, where the first of the volunteer lifesaving teams began, which eventually evolved into the modern-day Great Lakes Coast Guard. The Life-Saving Service was a group of the hardiest men of their time. When a ship was spotted in distress, they manned lifeboats (large rowboats) and rowed out to the floundering vessel, rescuing all they could. They were integral in keeping the lake from claiming more lives than it did. This area is part of the famed shipwreck coast that runs from Grand Marais to Whitefish Point. Eventually, several of these Life-Saving Service stations sprouted up along this section of Lake Superior. A historical marker and old foundations reveal the spot.

From here one can do many things to enjoy the area at any time of the year. The river and surrounding land is excellent for any kind of activity. Of course, the fishing here is some of the best for trout and has heavy late-year salmon runs. Also, several inland lakes within 5 miles of the Two Hearted River have northern pike, muskellunge, walleye, and bass, and all of these small lakes have public accesses with primitive campgrounds. The usual abundance of facilities and low fishing pressure give fishermen a rare opportunity.

Though more famous for fishing, the area boasts so many other things to do. Because of all the logging in the area— I said I'd get to this—an extraordinary diversity of wildlife exists. An abundance of black bear, deer, and game birds make this a hunter's paradise too.

A by-product of the logging is a vast number of trails that access many places otherwise unreachable. Hundreds of miles of trails are just waiting to be explored by four-wheelers (on most trails you don't even need that), motorcycles, bicycles, hikers, or backpackers. The North Country Hiking Trail runs through here. Winter here provides unlimited snowmobiling, cross-country skiing, and snowshoeing, or winter camping and backpacking possibilities if you're hardy enough to take it. The all-year recreation area that can be used for any kind of outdoor recreation. .

Located at the mouth of the river is an establishment called the Rainbow Lodge. If you really don't want to stay at the campground or it's the wrong time of the year and you don't want to rough it, the Rainbow Lodge has accommodations. You get a nice size room, which includes double bed, couch that folds out into a sleeper, kitchen table, bathroom with shower, sink, range, dishes, pots, pans, and utensils. You have to bring your own cooler. It's like renting a small efficiency apartment. It's a good deal for the money and the hosts are very accommodating.

A paddle down the Two Hearted River is one of the absolute highlights of the area, the finest way to relax and get the feel for the charm of the river. The Two Hearted has been a staple for Upper Peninsula paddlers for years. Three basic paddles result in two to three hours, four to six hours, or two to three days to complete. Canoe camps are located along the river for the last of the three. On the canoe trip I took, I saw one of these camps. They are nice, well-kept facilities with fire pits, outhouses, and water pumps. This is a classic trip for any time of year except winter, of course. There are snowmobiling trails to cover the winter season.

Where the Big Two Hearted River meets Lake Superior. (top)
The Big Two Hearted River as it nears Lake Superior. Across that bridge is where the Two Hearted Life Saving Station once stood. (middle)
Boy on a rope (bottom)

A trip to the Two Hearted is well worth the effort any time of the year, but it's a real playground for in the fall. Go visit what captivated Hemingway so. You'll end up like him and be back again and again. More info at http://pointsnorth-books.com/sites

Black River
Gogebic County

M uch can be said about the many magnificent and wonderful waterfalls throughout Michigan's Upper Peninsula. The Black River in Gogebic County is no exception. Showcasing seven falls in a 6-mile stretch, no other falls are like them in character, makeup, or abundance. It is an extraordinary place any time of the year and is well worth a journey to see them.

The Black River is located 15 miles north of Bessemer off U.S. Route 2 on County Road 513. County Road 513 parallels the river for 6 miles before entering the Black River Park. Trails leading to the various falls can be accessed from this road. In addition, the North Country Trail has incorporated this trail system into its system. It is well maintained.

All the falls are accessible, but some are definitely easier to get to than others. Distance is marked at the beginning of each trail, so you can decide right away if you're up to the hike.

For about nine miles, the trail takes the hiker through the woods and along the gorges that make up the Black River. In the north 6-mile section, seven separate waterfalls make this hike worth the effort. Alternate trails run off the main trail to the road at individual waterfall sites. So the trail system is quite versa-

Black River wild river

tile; a visitor can view as much of the area as he or she chooses. The falls can be taken in a day or over the course of a few. They can fit any plan.

An underused 30-site campground at the end of County Road 513 is at the Black River Harbor, at the mouth of the river on Lake Superior. The highly picturesque and well-sheltered bay has been tastefully developed into a multiuse recreation area. The park itself is

The Black River Harbor, which connects to Lake Superior, is a harbor of refuge where boats can get to safety during Lake Superior's temperamental moods.

open seasonally, as is the campground. This campground is well maintained. It has electric hookups but no showers or modern out facilities. The sites are well spread out, so a small amount of privacy can be maintained. A small per-night fee is the only cost.

The harbor of refuge can accommodate all size boats from Lake Superior. A large-craft launch sits in the harbor too. A small store, open seasonally, provides refreshments (not groceries) and fuel. Any type of supplies should be picked up before leaving Bessemer.

A trail that leads over the river, via a long suspension bridge, eventually ends up on a Lake Superior beach. The beach, which is nicely secluded with good swimming in the summer, is one of the nicest places on the shoreline.

This area has special appeal anytime of the year. Though the campground is open on a seasonal basis, the county road is plowed and accessible all year. Each season takes on its own special characteristics, and the Black River reflects them well.

Spring and fall herald trout and salmon runs, and the river is well known for seasonal fishing. Brook trout fishing is possible, but because of the steepness of the Black River Gorge the fisherman should be part mountain goat and warned to take caution. The harbor makes deepwater fishing easy on Superior in an underfished section.

The most unique season here is winter. Because it is accessible, the Black River presents some of the most breathtaking cross-country skiing and snowshoeing there is. The series of waterfalls, when frozen, creates dazzling ice formations and sculptures that overpower the senses with one winter vision after another.

One can make an excellent side trip to the Black River area when visiting for some of the other big winter activities. On County Road 513 on the way to the Black River is Copper Peak ski flying hill and Big Powderhorn Mountain Resort for skiing. The Black River attractions are great alternatives to

Gorge Falls (top)
Conglomerate Falls (bottom)

Rainbow Falls (top)
Potawatomi Falls (bottom)

doing the same thing all the time. Actually, when visiting any of the several Bessemer-Ironwood ski resorts (there are several) a ride to the river is never far.

The Black River shouldn't be missed when travelling the Upper Peninsula. Vacant campsites are always available, with few visitors at any one time. The quiet and spectacular surroundings make for a classic Upper Peninsula experience. For more information, see http://www.superiortrails.com/black-river-mi.html and http://www.fishweb.com/ maps/gogebic/waterfalls/blackrv_parkway/map.html or visit http://pointsnorthbooks.com/sites

Author's Note: Be sure to go to the Black River in the Bessemer area of Gogebic County. At least three Black Rivers are in the Upper Peninsula. Other Black River Falls exist as well.

Brevort Lakes Mackinac County

Brevort Lake fishing.

L akes are abundant in the U.P., but the natural beauty and serenity of the two Brevort Lakes set them apart from others. Tucked away in the woods near the Lake Michigan shore and only a few miles down the road west of St. Ignace and the Mackinaw Straits, they provide the visitor a taste of the deep-woods experience without the hassle of crowds or a long trail to get there. If you are in desperate need of a serious, relaxing getaway, visiting the Brevort Lakes area could be the answer.

The two, Little and Big Brevort Lakes, also known as the Brevoort Lake Recreation Area, are located near the town of Brevort, on U.S. Route 2. The area is filled with attractions for the traveler and has historical significance. The Brevort Lakes area provides an inexpensive and pleasant base camp for trips to the Straits or Mackinac Island.

Little Brevort Lake

The smaller of the two lakes, Little Brevort Lake lies on the northeast side of the town of Brevort. This quiet, serene lake is nestled in a secluded hollow, a peaceful, restive camping area.

The campground is reached by turning off U.S. Route 2 at the town of

Little Brevort Lake

Brevort—a well-marked turn. Travel north 1 mile and turn right. Follow the road 1 more mile, and the entrance is on the right, easily visible.

The 20 campsites are cut into an aromatic, thick cedar grove. The road circles down to the lakeshore and public access. Bubbling among the cedars is an artesian well with delicious, ice-cold water. This sheltered spot is ideal for fishing, canoeing, and rowboating. For hikers and backpackers, an excellent hiking trail runs in either direction from the camp around the lake for 2.5 miles. A walk to the top of the ridge reveals a panoramic view of the lake. The hiking here is especially nice.

This campground experiences minimal use. Most is by fishermen, so the surrounding area remains unworn and scenic, maintaining a wilderness feel. If fishing is a priority, don't pass up the opportunity here. The Michigan Department of Natural Resources (D.N.R.) maintains the campground and keeps the lake well stocked with most Michigan warm-water fish.

Regardless of your favorite outdoor activity, you'll enjoy camping at Little Brevort Lake. For more information check out the D.N.R. webpage: http://www.michigandnr.com/parksandtrails/Details.aspx?id=691&type=SFCG or via http://pointsnorthbooks.com/sites

Big Brevort Lake

Located 5 miles east of Brevort is Brevoort Lake Recreation Area on Big Brevort Lake. (Yes, the name is spelled both ways.) The entrance off U.S. Route 2 is easy to find. This campground is built and maintained by the U.S. Forest Service. It is one of the nicest in the U.P., with showers, running water, and hookups. About seventy sites are heavily used at times, but vacancies are usu-

Brevort Lake camping.

ally available. This campground, too, is situated in a scenic spot on a beautiful lake, which is dotted by camps and cottages.

Fishing is popular, as are water sports like waterskiing and sailboarding. Restrictions on motor size may apply, so check with the U.S. Forest Service if you're not sure whether your boat would qualify.

Big Brevort Lake Campground is ideal for all family members, especially those who don't enjoy roughing it. Among the well-kept, clean, modern facilities is a playground for children. A nature trail meanders through the wilderness, offering photo shots of varied habitats. Only a mile away rests a stretch of Lake Michigan beach open to the public for swimming. For more information, go to the USFS website: http://www.fs.usda.gov/recarea/hiawatha/recarea/?recid=13292 or via http://pointsnorthbooks.com/sites

Little Brevort Lake artesian well.

The next time a weekend is available for a mini-vacation, consider Brevort Lakes for fun and relaxation. It's easy to find and close to supplies. The town of Brevort and surrounding area contain many stores and tourist attractions. The rates are inexpensive, making this a most economical way to see local attractions.

Canyon Falls Roadside Park
Baraga County

Sturgeon River.

One of the real benefits of travel-ling throughout Michigan is its roadside parks. Often affording views of many of Michigan's natural wonders, they are always worth a stop. In the Upper Peninsula this also holds true, especially at a roadside park in Baraga County called Canyon Falls.

The Canyon Falls Roadside Park is located 14 miles east of L'Anse on U.S. Route 41. Located on the south side of the road, the park has only one turn-in instead of the usual two. Keep in mind that because the area is a roadside park, no overnight camping is allowed. Nev-ertheless, spending time here should be mandatory, as one of the magnifi-cent sights of the Upper Peninsula hides here in the wilderness.

A well-marked path leads from the parking lot downhill and into the woods. Take it. The well-traveled, wind-ing trail leads through old-growth ce-dars and pines. Boardwalks bridge over springs and sensitive areas. Before long, the Sturgeon River appears through the trees as it cuts through the Upper Peninsula wilderness. Large flat rocks along the riverbank provide natural places to sit and take in the beauty of the river.

Ahead, the trail makes a slight rise, and, without warning, the sound of the crashing water of Canyon Falls suddenly fills the air. The waterfall is here, and so is the canyon that gives the falls its name. Canyon Falls is the beginning of the Sturgeon River Gorge Wilderness, a treacherous and thick wilderness area.

The trail ends here—but what an ending! Ancient trees grow out of stone cliffs. Rainbows project across the rushing water of the falls in the sunshine. Downstream, the sheer rock cliffs rise where the river has cut through them for ten thousand years. The mist from the falls keeps the rocks damp and colorful. Springs flow from the cliffs, feeding the river that runs below. "Worth the walk" betrays the splendor of the scene; it is much more than that.

Few places are like Canyon Falls. Most will find the trail fairly easy, young and old. Only about 20 minutes or less are needed to get back there—very little time relative to the reward that waits. To truly round out a visit here, make sure to pack a picnic. Tables at the park are nicely placed under large old-growth shade trees.

A hike, a picnic, breathtaking scenery—what's not to like? Canyon Falls Roadside Park is one of those hidden gems that most wish they could find. Don't pass it by.

For more information about Canyon Falls Roadside Park check here: https://www.michigan.org/property/canyon-falls or via http://pointsnorth-books.com/sites

At the falls (top)
Beginning of gorge (middle)
Mikel at cedar tree shelter (bottom)

Cornish Pump and Mining Museum and World War II Glider Museum Dickinson County

Iron Mountain, Michigan, exudes iconic Upper Peninsula history. A drive through the town quickly reinforces that impression. The city still maintains 80 percent of its original buildings, and if one looks closely, new construction is often atop the remains of an old mining operation or mine-tailings pile. Though iron mining is not unusual in the Upper Peninsula past, Iron Mountain's solutions to its problems has it standing alone in the nation's history.

A hundred years ago, it took a big machine to do a big job. The bigger the job, the bigger the machine was made to handle it. The Cornish Pump in Iron Mountain is such a big machine. A monument to bygone days and state-of-the-art technology, it and the surrounding museum are one of Iron Mountain's most enjoyable and educational attractions.

Iron Mountain, like the name implies, was one of the hubs of early Upper Peninsula iron mining. The activity was fierce and profitable, with the city growing out of it. Mines dotted the

Cornish Pump Museum building

surrounding landscape. One of these, the Chapin Mine, was the richest ore-producing mine on the Lake Superior range and one of the richest in the world. But, there was a serious problem with the mine. The shafts ran directly beneath a cedar swamp, which created extreme water problems for the mine. Flooding was constant. The working conditions for the miners were horrible and dangerous. Lost production time due to impassable shafts was tremendous. Something had to be done.

PEWABIC MINE, IRON MOUNTAIN, MICHIGAN, CA. 1910
WILLIAM JOSEPH TRESTRAIL AND MINING PARTNER WITH CANDLESTICKS
AND OILERS (MINING CLOTHING)

Cornish Pump Museum mining floor exhibit (top left)
Mining Museum with historical miners (top right)
World War II Glider Museum exhibit (bottom)

The mine owners came to the conclusion that they needed an immense pump similar to that used in Cornwall, England, in the tin mines to solve water problems. The E.P. Allis Company from Milwaukee, Wisconsin (of the eventual Allis-Chalmers fame), was commissioned to design and build its version of what was called a Cornish pumping engine. In 1891, the colossal creation was erected above the Chapin Mine. The finished product stood over 54 feet high and was estimated to weigh 725 tons. It kept three mines dry with a capability of pumping up to 5 million gallons of water a day and completely revolutionized mining for the three mines. For many years it stood as the dominating feature on Iron Mountain's skyline.

Today, the building housing the pump and the museum no longer stand in prominence, but the breathtaking relic

The pump at Cornish Pump Museum (top)
Mining exhibit (bottom)

the centerpiece for one of the area's finest mining exhibits. Displays tell the tale of every aspect of iron mining on the Eastern Menominee Range.

The museum is located on the north side of Iron Mountain on Kent Street. It's situated two blocks west from U.S. Route 2, and signs on the highway show the way. A gift shop greets the visitor near the entrance; the small admission fee is paid there. Students aged 11 to 20 pay less, and children under 10 are free.

The walls are lined with display after display, an amazing collection of the odd and curious. Through photos, newspaper clippings, tools, clothing, models, drawings, and equipment, visitors experience Iron Mountain mining. The Cornish Pump sits in the center of the room, overshadowing all else. The deeply researched displays tell the history of mining while vividly depicting its harsh realities.

A back room is filled with exhibits , such as a collection of the larger essentials of mining like ore carts, railroad cars, ore conveyors, and pulleys. Objects occupy every available space.

Mining in some way created the majority of communities in the U.P., and especially Iron Mountain. Nowhere else on the continent stands a Cornish pumping engine. It shows by its existence the magnitude of wealth in ore and manpower that went into literally carving this community out of the surrounding landscape.

A step through the back door leads to the second museum in the complex, the World War II Glider and Military Museum. Planes hang from the ceiling, and antique Ford vehicles are set on display. Wall displays are dedicated to Iron Mountain and Kingsford area veterans.

In the early days, Henry Ford established an auto plant in Kingsford, a twin city to Iron Mountain. When the

is preserved and protected for all to view. The mammoth piece of machinery, which used to be housed in an old brownstone building, is now surrounded by a newer corrugated steel structure and museum artifacts. No longer pumping water for the mines, it is now

A glider at World War II Glider Museum

mining industry was on its decline, Ford's auto plant gave Dickinson County extended life.

A section of this museum displays wonderful old restored vintage Fords, including a magnificent "woody" from the early days. Most of Ford's wood vehicles and wood parts were produced throughout the Upper Peninsula.

The display follows Ford vehicles into the late 1930s and early 1940s. Like most American factories during World War II, the Kingsford factory was part of the war effort and retooled to produce planes. A huge World War II glider sits in a large portion of the room! Consisting of little more than wood and cloth, this plane was made for covert and silent operations. The missions were frequently fatal, and few such planes survived more than one. Death rode as a constant companion on board these flimsy planes.

The Kingsford Ford plant made these gliders, hence the association with the museum and the Ford Motor Company displays. This plane has to be seen to be believed. The museum does an excellent job of conveying not only the importance of these gliders to the war effort but also the near-suicidal conditions of flying in one.

The future of this complex looks promising. Along with the Cornish Pump and World War II Glider museums, another museum has been added,—the Menominee Range Historical Museum, Formerly downtown in one of the old historical buildings, the Menominee Range Historical Foundation has moved the museum, creating a museum complex unparalleled in the Upper Peninsula in placing all aspects of the region's history in one place.

Author's Note: When this entry was first researched, the Menominee Range Museum had not moved yet and was not a part of the complex. Hence the lack of description of it. Consequently, a visit to the Cornish Pump will give visitors an opportunity to visit something that I haven't seen yet. Surprise!

For more information on the museums of Iron Mountain or its history visit www.menomineerangehistoricalfoundation.org or via http://pointsnorthbooks.com/sites

Donnelley Wilderness Tract
Marquette County

Dedication sign (left)
The Little Garlic River, one of the midwest's finest trout streams. (right)

A wall of trees lines the dirt parking area. Ahead stands a sign next to a trail, beaconing like a doorway to another world. And maybe that's exactly what it is, a world rarely experienced. The sign says, "Elliott Donnelley Wilderness Tract: This land along the Little Garlic River was presented to the people of Michigan by Elliott Donnelley of Chicago on behalf of Trout Unlimited. His gift assures that this wild watershed will forever be preserved for those who cherish fishing for trout in the pure waters of their natural habitat as god so intended." Indeed, that invitation is hard to ignore.

Situated in the foothills of the Huron Mountains in northern Marquette County, the Little Garlic River basin and the surrounding area are typical of the mountain lands. This area of rugged beauty and wild surroundings is known as the Donnelley Wilderness Tract, a pristine place that will satisfy the hardened outdoorsman or the novice just looking for a momentary taste of primordial Upper Peninsula forest.

The Elliott Donnelley Wilderness Tract was donated to the State of Michigan for the express purpose of having a beautiful and natural environment for the stream fisherman. Mr. Donnelley's wish has been fulfilled and then some. In providing a place for the fisherman, he has also created a quiet and serene public area that can cater to nearly anyone's outdoor preference. The tract consists of approximately 3 square miles that cover more than half of the entire Little Garlic basin. It makes for a year-round playground that goes largely unused.

To get to the tract, travel 16 miles north of Marquette on County Road 550. After crossing the Little Garlic River bridge, the turnout for the tract is immediately on the left. The bridge identifying the river is unmarked, but a vast open field is on the right-hand side, and four lanes begin here. If you miss the turnout, a Department of Natural Resources access road is about 100 feet beyond on the left-hand side of the road. The department's road to the tract is too rough for the average vehicle to travel. Turn around here and go back to the turnout.

Although no campgrounds are here, "leave no trace" camping is allowed. This is another of those wilderness tracts where public use is encouraged and it costs nothing but your time and effort. Hiking trails honeycomb the area; they run along the river bed or take the hiker up on the high ridges and bluffs. Hiking here is reminiscent of hiking in the Porcupine Mountains in that the trails are of the same type and quality. With open camping, lengthy backpacking explorations are possible, which allow one to really enjoy some of the primeval growth that abounds throughout the basin. Day hikes are also rewarding, and for educational nature walks, this place is hard to beat. Much diversity of vegetation and habitat allow possibilities of seeing and identifying divergent species of plants and animals. If you're a photographer or bird watcher, this area is a must. The main trail here is part of the North Country Hiking Trail and is well marked.

The trail through the Donnelly Wilderness is lined with hardwoods and tall forest.

For easier hiking, the DNR access road provides a very interesting and scenic hike. It meanders past high rock bluffs and through stands of hardwoods and pines. About a half mile along the road, the ruins of old homesteads stand, mostly collapsed, reminding us of the hard days of U.P. pioneer life. This road is also a quicker way for a hiker to get deeper back into the basin. The ambitious hiker can reach Little Garlic Falls. Be advised that the falls are a long way back, about 3.5 miles, one way and is hard walking to be reached in a day. This access road has many trails that shoot off into dozens of different areas. On occasional pull-offs, former campsites offer already cleared and usable camps.

There are many overlooks along the trail giving spectacular views of the Little Garlic valley. (left)
Into the wilderness (right)

The seasons bring different aspects to the Donnelley experience. Spring brings the annual rainbow trout run that the Little Garlic is so famous for and is also the only time of the year with any kind of heavy use of the area. A lot of fishermen come here and their trip is always worthwhile. The fishing really is the best here. The river has a reputation with sportsmen as one of the finest in the Midwest. The Little Garlic is a year-round designated trout stream.

Summer brings good hiking and brook trout fishing. Wildlife is at its densest this time of year. The season offers some of the best opportunities for photographers. Be forewarned, though—a high bug population makes precautions necessary. Otherwise, you too will be in misery.

Fall here can be nothing short of breathtaking. A vast diversity of hardwoods and pines are mixed well, giving a color experience ranked as one of the most brilliant. Also, hunting here is excellent. Grouse, woodcock, deer, squirrels, rabbits, and bears have habitat here, and their numbers flourish. The Donnelley can be an excellent place to set up hunting camps for a different and rare hunting trip.

Winter turns the place into a playground. You can do anything here. Snowshoeing can be a completely new and rare venture. Winter camping is very pleasant because sheltering grottos and bluffs are everywhere and the dense trees keep the wind to a minimum, making for cozy and protected camps. Cross-country skiing can be done on the foot trails or on the access road.

The Tract will make for a rugged and wild Upper Peninsula experience no matter what kind of exploring fits your fancy. Something new and scenic to see awaits around every corner. The real beauty of the Donnelley is its untamed wild terrain. Spending time here will renew and restore you. More info at http://pointsnorthbooks.com/sites

Drummond Island Chippewa County

In Michigan's Upper Peninsula, the "Far East" doesn't mean the Orient, Buddhism, or rickshaws. It means small resorts, tucked away campsites, wilderness trails, and outstanding hunting and fishing. It means Drummond Island, one of the most interesting and secluded places in the U.P.. Drummond Island is the largest island in the Great Lakes in U.S. territory, containing 137 square miles, much of which is state land and open to the public. The possibilities are endless.

The island is the eastern most point in the Upper Peninsula, located east of the Straits of Mackinac. To get there, go north of the Mackinac Bridge on I-75 for 15 miles, then head east on M-134 for 40 miles to Village of DeTour.

Right away the fun starts aboard a car ferry to Drummond Island. Not many of these are left in Michigan; they're a rare treat. You drive on at DeTour and drive off at Drummond, never leaving your car. The ferry runs year round. If the route gets too iced-in during winter, the ice becomes a road.

Once on the island, The small community of Drummond has paved roads, with cottages, private homes, and resorts tucked away in quiet and scenic corners. The peaceful island seems detached and unconcerned with the rest

Sunset

of the world. That's what makes a stay here so pleasant, the feeling of being away from everything.

Hunting and fishing on the island is legendary. The bays produce record catches of perch and walleye, while inland lakes

The shoreline of Drummond Island hides a place steeped in history and opportunity.

are well stocked with trophy bass and pike. Game is plentiful, with healthy populations of all Michigan game animals including black bear, deer, and ruffed grouse. Varied waterfowl seem to nest heavily. To really make your stay interesting, throughout the island are fishing and hunting resorts that, besides producing private and fully equipped cabins, have guide, boat, and bait services, which can be rented or chartered. This island caters to the outdoorsmen..

Drummond Island is full of trails, hidden lakes, and wilderness. Backpackers, paddlers, bicyclists, horsepackers, and ORV enthusiasts are at home here. The island has year-round activities, so snowmobilers, cross-country skiers, and snowshoers will equally delight in the possibilities. The trails wind deep into the unpopulated interior of the north and east, which is remote and thick. Additionally, people can see spectacular fall and spring beauty here.

Summer brings bugs, and preparation is a must. Winter provides snowmobile touring that leaves virtually all areas accessible. Photography opportunities are breathtaking; a trip to the island should always include a camera. On the far eastern end of the island are fossil ledges that reflect a prehistoric past.

Drummond's rich and intriguing history shows it has always been a place of refuge and escape. Settling began when the British were forced to retreat from Mackinac in 1812 but still had to maintain control of the upper Great Lakes. A large Indian meeting place and ceremonial ground was in the area, so control and protection was a prime concern. The massacre at Fort Michilimackinac a few years earlier had made them wary. A rich fur trade in the U.P. provided the king with wealth he wasn't going to give up. In order to maintain British grip on the upper waterway, soldiers retreated and established a fort on Drummond Island on a high hill that overlooked where DeTour is today and the channel in between. This fort was fully garrisoned for about ten years. After that, it was abandoned when Drummond Island was ruled to be U.S. territory.

Then the island lay unused for a few years until a Mormon named Seaman built the first permanent homestead, fleeing persecution from Beaver Island.

Paddling the countless islands that surround Drummond is a paddlers dream come true. Exploring these is a treat not found in most places. (top)

The township campground on Drummond Island situated on Potagannissing Bay has breathtaking views of the dozens of islands that dot the area. (bottom left)

Remnants of the island's history can be found when exploring Drummond. (bottom right)

Mormons established a settlement at Beaver Island, but they were driven off because their leader had declared himself king and the U.S. Government was unhappy with that. Thinking that Drummond Island could give them a new foothold and peace at last, Seaman took his family and settled on Drummond. Soon more refugee Mormons followed. Then non-Mormons trickled in and other small settlements began to be carved out of the harsh environment. Again the Mormons found themselves in a battle for religious survival. Prejudice from the outsiders eventually manifested itself in religious debates and arguments. In the end, Mormons lost the fight, as they were driven away once again.

Eventually, dolomite was discovered and a mine opened up. Suddenly, Drummond Island had come into its own. Dolomite mining is the only actual industry there, and it still operates today. The mine is the first thing a visitor sees when arriving on the car ferry. The entire island economy revolves around this mine and tourism.

This rich history and the hard realities of settling the island are aptly depicted at the Drummond Island Historical Museum. Nice displays give a wonderful and vivid overview of the settling and progress that has taken place. This is perhaps the best way to get a feel for the island, the people, and the way of life here. Displays of models,

Another relic of the past. This is an abandoned sawmill that reflects the lumbering past of Drummond Island.

artifacts, photos, and clippings are set out so that the viewer takes a trip along a timeline that leads to an eye-opening understanding of the descendants of these hardy and determined pioneers.

For the explorers out there, a drive along some of the roads will take you to locations of some of the original island settlements and past standing and ruined homesteads. These monuments of the past can be seen struggling to survive within the growth of the countryside.

Accommodations on the island are varied, from the many resorts to the couple of motels. A campground is 6 miles from the ferry landing off the main road, with the turnoff well marked on the northeast side of the road. The cost to camp is small. The campground provides electrical hookups but nothing else—no shower or sewer facilities. The place inhabits a sheltered cove on Potagannissing Bay, which consists of a rocky shoreline on the south side of the island. On the whole, the campground is nice, but it gets very little use. About 75 sites are reasonably spread out, providing privacy and quiet. Small boats can be launched here, but midsize and larger boats have to use one of the dozen other sites found elsewhere.

Paddling Potagannissing Bay in my kayak was one of the highlights of my stay. Countless islands big and small make paddling here an experience like no other. Beware—the winds pick up quickly and can be dangerous.

Drummond Island is a self-sufficient community, so people find many supplies, such as gas and groceries. Excellent restaurants populate the area, including a Mexican diner that is a highlight of the island. Drummond Island is a growing community with new businesses and recreational opportunities developing all the time. A new tall ship has made its home on the island and is available for rides and hire. The island can provide a visit both satisfying and memorable.

One closing tip—pick up a Chamber of Commerce map to help your stay. It shows all the backroads and points of interest. For further information, call or write the Drummond Island Chamber of Commerce at Drummond Island, MI 49726 or visit http://pointsnorthbooks. com/sites

Eben Ice Caves
Alger County

D og sleds, skis, snowshoes, and hiking—I've seen all methods used to get to the Eben Ice Caves in Eben Junction, Michigan. Though the trail is not long, it's far enough to make a fun winter jaunt by any method you use. The attraction is one of the best prescriptions for cabin fever. After viewing the Eben Ice Caves, one of the highlights of Michigan's Upper Peninsula natural winter wonders, you will feel awed by winter's artistry. If you get out at all in the snow, this should be one of your mandatory destinations.

Nineteen miles southwest of Munising on M-94, or 29 miles southeast of Marquette, in Alger County is Eben Junction. As the name implies, it is little more than a crossroads with a few homes clustered nearby. The attraction of the caves is known by all of the locals, and they are willing to give directions to the exact location. A bar and a store are on the corner, and the people in each place are friendly and informative. To get there, turn north from this corner and go about a mile and a half to where the road turns 90 degrees to the right. Go around the turn and follow the road another half mile until the next 90-degree turn, and park. You will face an open pasture.

Exterior with figure

Walk through an open, old wooden gateway into the field. The footpath begins there, and all modes of cross-country winter travel are used on this trail, which is packed hard enough for easy walking. I've gone several times and was always able to walk it on foot with never any struggle or sinking.

Exterior view   Interior

The trail goes straight across the pasture and enters woods of virtually all maple. An occasional yellow birch or elm makes an appearance, but such trees are very few and far apart. The walking path slopes gently as the trail meanders between the tall, straight hardwoods. One can easily picture the dense foliage the area must have in the summer, but still it wouldn't have the ever-present feeling of freshness and clarity that comes only from a winter day.

Continuing its downward trend, the trail turns and reveals an old log cabin on the left, a hunting shack that seems still sometimes used. The door is locked and not open to the public, but the cabin makes for a bonus sight along the way. The log work is hand-hewn and in a traditional one-room style—a small example of the old UP. The cabin marks the halfway point to the main attraction.

Past the cabin, the trail dips again and enters a lush cedar thicket. It winds among the greenery, adding new colors and wonderful smells into the winter air. The forest floor is covered with snowshoe hare tracks. Walk quietly, and chances are good that, with an observant eye, you'll see several. Their white coat makes excellent camouflage.

As you walk farther, you will emerge from this collection of cedars, and on the left is a steep ridge while the trail leads to some large trees—some of the largest I've seen in the U.P. The trail skirts the ridge for a few yards and then suddenly you will stand on the edge. Looking down, a panorama of ice spreads below your feet.

There, in a rock grotto, are the ice caves. The long thick icicles have taken on mineral colors. The trail descends sharply from here, and a long, thick rope for handhold is strung between the trees to the bottom. The trail stops in front of the ice formations that hang twenty feet long or more.

They're formed, hundreds of them clustered together, in brown, tan, beige, blue, and white. The sight is breathtaking. Water can be heard running over and through them, which doesn't seem possible this time of year. But the spring water's flow is the required ingredient for this spectacle of Mother Nature's finest winter artistry.

Some fallen pieces of ice lie like broken Roman columns at a ruined city. Some of the spectators try to see shapes in the ice like some people do with clouds. Walking inside the cave is like stepping into a wonderland. Nooks and crannies exhibit intricate formations highlighted by freshly blown snow. Some ice is newly born, still forming, while old ones dangle broken and lie shattered.

The grotto that all of this is continually created in is situated halfway up on a ridge that descends 200 yards into a stream that runs below. The location is utterly picturesque in every aspect. The sandstone and shale wall that makes up the rear half of the caves curves inward while the spring water trickles from the top, so although tons of ice are building down the front, the concave wall allows one to walk behind the ice as if walking behind some waterfalls. Walking between the ice and rock wall is an unusual if not a slightly eerie experience, but this is what creates the cave effect—one side ice and the other rock.

Upon entering the cave, I noticed a definite temperature drop. Though everything is water and stone, there was no musty smell; the air was fresh and clean. Constantly water can be heard

Ice stalactites

running and splashing over the ice. Small tunnels of ice run in random directions. The formations are shaped just like limestone stalactites and stalagmites. Countless tiny ones make up the whole of the large ones. The natural intricacies are wonderfully beautiful, especially in the sunlight, though beauty is always there and breathtaking no matter what type of weather. One of the things that struck me the most was the realization that in non-winter months the water flow is a small stream less than a foot wide.

Because the water is always flowing, the ice is always building and changing throughout the year, so more than one trip a year can bring new things each time. This is one of the U.P.'s winter wonders, so go see it. Don't forget the camera! More info at http://pointsnorth-books.com/sites

Fortune Lakes, Bewabic Historical State Park Iron County

The beach and lake at Bewabic State Park.

A visit to the Fortune Lakes reveals a fortune in beauty, relaxation, activities and fun. Most parks establish around some local event or location. On the shore of Fortune Lakes, Bewabic State Park has made its own history.

The Fortune Lakes resort area consists of four lakes interconnected by natural waterways, allowing miles of on-the-water touring and a treasure of scenery and wildlife. Some private resorts are around Fortune Lakes, but people have been coming to one campground for nearly one hundred years—Bewabic State Park, one of only two in Upper Michigan that remain open year round.

The park and the Fortune Lakes are located 4 miles west of Crystal Falls on U.S. Route 2. Bewabic has a well-groomed yet rustic campground nestled on the shore of Fortune Lake. Exactly 137 campsites are carved out of 315 acres of forest. The facilities cater to the active vacationer, who will be treated to accommodations and hospitality.

Bewabic Park, established in 1923, is one of the earliest established parks in Michigan, and it is on the National Register of Historic Places. During the 1930s a crew from the Civilian Conservation Corps (C.C.C.) created a playground with rustic works of art. They took a small peninsula, dredged a canal through it, and created a picnic island with stone cooking grills that look like a small chimney. An architect hired from Ironwood named Abraham Anderson designed a log bath house that shines with a pine interior. Even the restrooms received special attention and were built as gothic stone buildings. The park was designed to be relaxing and pleasant for every age. All of this stands today unchanged. Even the old tennis courts remain among the huge pines. (Bewabic is the only state park in Michigan with tennis courts.) The park was popular with locals and those traveling to the region. It was successful enough that the State of Michigan purchased it in 1966 during an expansion of the state-park system.

Park accommodations include tennis courts, a beach, bathroom and shower facilities, two playgrounds, and public access for boats. A day area is available for those who wish to spend a few hours but not camp.

The park has a 1.5-mile nature trail, an attraction any time during the year. It follows the shoreline then meanders off into the thick woods. In the winter, it serves as an excellent cross-country ski or snowshoe trail.

The lakes, of course, are the main attraction. Their interconnection provides adventurous yet safe canoeing. Visitors can spend days exploring the waterways with kayaks or boats or via snowmobile after they've frozen over.

The lakes have a wealth of fish—walleye, perch, bluegill, and bass—and fishing is excellent year round. Visitors can rent canoes and boats, and bait is available at several places nearby.

The Paint River flows about 3 miles north of the park. If you stay at Bewabic, a trip to the Paint River should be a priority, as it offers spectacular sights that are easily accessible. The first attraction is Chicagon Falls, a torrent of cascading water both gorgeous and breathtaking. Another of the river's offerings is Horserace Rapids, a chaotic sight. The wild, rushing, churning water is a wonder to behold.

Tennis court (top)
CCC stone building (middle)
Group pavilion (bottom)

Viewing the Rapids and Falls is great in the winter—the natural ice sculpting is no less than magnificent. A trip on snowshoes, skis, or snowmobile will be a memorable journey. The spring offers some of the best white-water paddling.

The State of Michigan owns hundreds of acres around the Paint River and Fortune Lakes, all open to the public. The game population is among the heaviest in Michigan, so hunting is encouraged. The many trails allow for days of off-roading and accessing remote areas.

With its wealth of activities and beautiful sights, the Fortune Lakes area offers rare jewels anytime of the year. Visit historical Bewabic State Park and the Fortune Lakes resort area to experience why so many have returned year after year for nearly a century. For more information, write Bewabic State Park, 720 Idlewild Rd. Crystal Falls, MI 49920, or phone 906- 524-7444 or visit http://pointsnorthbooks.com/sites

Grand Island for a Grand Time Alger County

Munising Bay is a beautiful and popular destination for travelers who want to see the finest that the Lake Superior basin can provide. Home of Pictured Rocks National Lakeshore, an unusual amount of waterfalls, the United States' only underwater preserve, and the majestic Grand Island, the bay is a rare place indeed. In May 1990, the U.S. Forest Service acquired Grand Island, and congress designated it as a National Recreation Area. Now much of the island is in public hands.

Most people see Grand Island from an overlook in Munising. Yet a side trip to the island can be a special experience. Williams Landing on Grand Island is one of the oldest place names on Lake Superior, and Abraham Williams and his wife were one of the first settlers to brave life on the Lake Superior frontier. The history here shaped life all along the Superior shoreline.

The 13,000-acre Grand Island, just across from Munising on the mainland, compliments Pictured Rocks, though it is not part of the national park. It is a separate entity under the control of the U.S. Forest Service and

Sunset (top)
Cemetery (bottom)

Trout Bay – west side (top)
Merchants Cabin (middle)
Thunder Cove overlook (bottom)

not the National Park Service. It is less known as a destination, which affords a much quieter experience for an individual or a family.

Established, primitive campsites are on the south end of the island at Murray and Trout Bays, within 2 miles of where the ferry puts in at Williams Landing. Tent sites populate the island all around, but in the summer months reservations are required. A couple of cabins can be rented; these are reasonably new and very nice to stay in.

Grand Island is a paradise for silent sports. Hiking, biking, and paddling are all encouraged. Trails crisscross the island, making most places of note easily accessible. Paddlers in Murray Bay may be interested in two shipwrecks in shallow water, visible from the surface. Buoys mark their locations.

Grand Island is designated as part of the Lake Superior Water Trail. One of the trails is a history loop that meanders through the settlement of Williams Landing. Many of the original old homes and homesteads still stand, and many of those are still lived in, so are not a part of the recreation area. The residents' privacy should be respected.

Abraham Williams and his family arrived on Grand Island in 1840. Williams felt that Sault Ste. Marie was too violent for his family. He became the first settler on Grand Island. He was invited to live there by a small tribe of natives that had used the island for their home for nearly 3 thousand years. They established a lucrative fur trade which made Grand Island an early hub of local commerce and made it a stopover and supply sta-

Mather Lodge

tion for those travelling the south shore of Lake Superior. It became a harbor of refuge in every sense of the words.

In time, the island evolved into a resort destination. The Williams Hotel, with its distinctive barn shape that makes it recognizable on the shore, was a destination for the rich and elite. It now is in private hands and can only be viewed from the water.

Because of the island's popularity, a tycoon by the name of William G. Mather decided he wanted Grand Island as the home for an ultimate hunting lodge. He purchased a large tract of land on the northwest side of the island and built a magnificent lodge on the shoreline. He then stocked his new game preserve with exotic game animals imported from around the world. Unfortunately many of them couldn't take the severe Lake Superior climate and died. The lodge was a failure. It still stands on the west side of Grand Island looking out over its own quiet bay.

During prohibition, the north side of the island was used for a dropping place for illegal booze. Bootleggers left casks of liquor in caves carved in the rocks. Later, someone from the mainland would pick it up when the coast was clear.

For many years, Cleveland-Cliffs Iron Company (C.C.I.), the company that Mather served as president, owned the island, and then the U.S. Forest Service took it over. Its mandate was to turn the island into an interpretive recreation area. The Forest Service has done just that. Highlighting the natural and the historic, Grand Island is a treat for the senses as well as the imagination. Signs placed throughout the island help interpret and visualize Grand Island and its past.

A ferry service runs from the mainland to the island from May to the beginning of October, for both passengers and gear, including bikes and kayaks. The ferry runs all day. Visitors can even rent gear right there at the ferry. The only vehicles allowed on the island belong to the residents and the U.S. Forest Service. Snowmobiles are allowed in the winter and ATVs only after October.

The two established campgrounds at Murray and Trout Bays have camping

Stone Quarry Cabin

sites, but camping is allowed throughout Grand Island at established tent sites. The U.S. Forest Service has made some incredible choices for site locations. Nowhere in the park is anyone far from a designated campsite. Water sources and pit toilets are also scattered about the island along the trails.

Grand Island has become a choice destination in winter for snowmobilers and cross-country skiers. Past winters have seen roughly three thousand visitors. From January through March, the bay is frozen solid, and access to the island is safe and simple. Powell Point, which is 1 mile west of Munising, is the closest access from the mainland, with only a half-mile jaunt across to Williams Landing on Grand Island. From there visitors are free to travel the seemingly endless miles of trails and roads that provide some of the finest winter fun the UP can offer.

Ice climbing has become the new, exciting winter sport that attracts quite a few enthusiasts in the winter. Many of the cliffs seep spring water, and in the frigid months, these freeze into giant ice columns. With the right kind of gear and skills, enthusiasts find the sport exhilarating, and new participants it up all the time.

Grand Island is like a small Isle Royale (an island on Lake Superior that contains a national park with surrounding smaller islands) that is a lot closer and easier to get to. It can be enjoyed in a day or as long as your time allows. It is a showplace for the natural variety and beauty so prevalent in the Munising area. No matter what time of year a visit is made, the island lives up to its name. From the immense ice formations that hang from the shoreline cliffs, to the intense fall colors that adorn the mixed hardwood and pine forest, to the lush colors of spring and summer, everchanging beauty will present something different every trip.

At the height of season, many campsites are available, and a day trip to the island to hike or bike can be a great way to get acquainted with the place. Go beyond the Munising overlook to experience the island firsthand. For more info http://pointsnorthbooks.com/sites

Iron County Historical Museum
Iron County

Museum entrance

t's like taking a trip in a time machine. When you step out of your car and begin walking around the grounds, you seem to be on an island isolated from the advances of time. Relics and buildings from the early days of the Upper Peninsula settlers surround the area, organized as an early typical community appeared. The Iron County Historical Museum has gone beyond the usual stereotypic museum. Known as a folk museum, it will change your perception of museums and history completely.

This particular folk museum is not only a journey through Iron County's past but also a look at what gives the Upper Peninsula its identity. Fourteen buildings on nearly eight acres all are filled with vi-

sions of the past, each being a historical piece. Demonstrations of folk and traditional arts and crafts take place throughout the year, as do ethnic festivals.

The museum is located 2 miles south of U.S. Route 2 at Iron River on County Road 424 at Caspian. It is open from mid-May to mid-September; the museum charges a small admission, but you will be overwhelmed by the displays. You could take days to view them all. To take in a fair amount of the open-air museum, you should set aside an entire day. Some picnic tables are on the grounds, so packing a lunch will make for a nice outing.

The headframe of the former Caspian Mine towers over everything and represents the heart and soul of the U.P. past in this region, the Menominee Iron Range. When the mine flooded, it stood derelict until the land was donated in the early 1960s to the Iron County Historical Society for it to use as a site for a museum. In the following years, the Historical Society has managed to save and display an unprecedented amount of local history.

Mining is only one facet of an extremely rich past. The main building, which is where visitors start their tour, is where the more traditional museum displays are set up. Many of the folk artists and craftsmen such as quilters, weavers, and traditional musical-instrument performers demonstrate their talents here.

Rows and rows of period antiques and clothing line the main building. Here, art exhibition rooms display works; particularly notable is the work of nationally famed wildlife artist Lee LeBlanc. Visitors can see originals and prints of nearly every piece turned out in his lifetime, including some work he did while employed by the Walt Disney Studios. He was one of the finest. Donations he made before he passed away of some of his artwork contributed heavily to the funding for the building of this museum. Examples of writing and artwork from several other local talents who have achieved notoriety grace the rooms—all of which is fascinating and enlightening.

Further along is Heritage Hall, which is filled with Native American exhibits, representing several large settlements of the area. The Mining Hall depicts Iron County mining history with outstanding working models that recreate all aspects of mining in its heyday; covered is the Caspian Mine, which stands outside the building.

Next is the Loom Room that shows weaving equipment. Hansen's Studio is an early photographer's display. Athletic Hall and the Sport's Shop show Iron

Logging diorama (top)
Diver display (middle)
Barber storefront (bottom)

County's Hall of Fame and a tribute to winter sports. Memorial Hall puts the effects of past wars on the area into perspective. The Type Shop, the Rum Rebellion Cellar, Professor Faverio's Music Studio, Oberg's Saloon, Skog's Beauty Shop, and the Fire Department are all different aspects of life from the past and packed full of artifacts to view. Few spaces are left empty.

From here visitors can delve more deeply and graphically into history as the typical feel of a museum fades away.

Village complex (top)
Caspian Mine (bottom)

es found in early living. Country school and chapel displays have artifacts from these establishments. The Dugout Room has several dugout canoes found in the area, and interspersed with them are mounted wildlife and Native American displays. Lastly, one of the more impressive exhibits, simply due to craftsmanship, is the Lumbering Hall and the Logging Camp. A miniature hand-carved model has to be seen to be believed. An injured logger took eight years to carve it; the model shows every aspect of lumbering camp life and work in the utmost detail. Nothing else is like it anywhere, and it is presumed to be the largest of its kind in the world. This is the last thing that the visitor sees in the main building.

Leaving that building, one walks to the Carrie Jacobs-Bond House, a 70-ton home that was moved onto the grounds. It is the former home of Miss Bond, who wrote dozens of songs such as "I Love You Truly" and "A Perfect Day." The entire home has been restored to the period from the 1880s to 1910, and much of the furniture and artifacts were Miss Bond's. It was an elegant house, and it remains that way.

A streetcar shed houses an immaculate car that ran in Iron River. The Stager Depot is a fully revived train depot with train cars waiting outside for freight. The box car is from 1917. The depot is full of railroad relics, such as a telegraph, old desks, stoves, benches and schedules. On the back waiting platform is a recreation of a depression scene from the 1930s and a rare artifact, a perpetual-motion machine.

Another treat is the 1920s gas station and pumps, situated next to the Shop's Building. Inside this is the old fire department with some original equipment and carts. Next to that is Fred's Barber Shop, dating back to the

Storefront windows reveal recreations of early store interiors, making the walk feel like a stroll through early downtown. The section is called the Village Green. It starts with Molly Pryne's Shop, a dressmaker's store. The Carpenter's Shop is filled with artifacts that come from many different cities of the U.P.. MacDonnel's Blacksmith Shop, Mercantile Store, Barber Shop, and Dr. Vilas's Drug Store are all part of this street walk.

A few other displays round out the building. A pioneer home display shows everyday utensils and applianc-

Homestead complex

1880s. The Pop Shop displays equipment from former area bottling works. Finally in the building is the Reporter Office, which houses some of the early machinery and tools of the early newspaper trade.

Several ore cars and remnants of mining equipment surround the Caspian Mine headframe. The old mine is the centerpiece of this historical community, as it surely was when it saw its heyday. The unusual piece in the exhibit is the large diamond drill rig.

The farming complex, an extensive acquisition for the museum, consists of nine actual homestead buildings preserved and converted to show various aspects of early pioneer life. They depict varying styles of homestead construction as well. One of the buildings has been converted to a working blacksmith shop. A log barn has been restored to store farm equipment and livestock, as well as hay and feed. A threshing barn with all the old, noisy threshing equipment in full working order provides quite the entertainment. Some grindstones from old mills exist here. Two homestead homes have been restored to depict living conditions from the 1800s. One even has

the old sauna next to it. A working sawmill with logging camp is another eye-opening and fascinating exhibit. A sleigh barn and harness room round out the area.

Those who have never had to be educated in a one-room schoolhouse will see something of what that was like in the full-sized and fully equipped schoolhouse on display. A church has been moved on site, redone to show the early religious experience.

Few museums have created what the Iron County Historical Society has with this museum. The unique experience reflects virtually every aspect of life in this highly historical region.

The Historical Society constantly adds to its already brimming displays, and every visit will reveal new things. The society prints up an annual schedule listing the demonstrations and festivals held on the grounds; therefore, you may wish to contact the society prior to a trip to plan for the events. Contact the museum by writing to the Iron County Historical and Museum Society, P.O. Box 272, 100 Brady Ave. Caspian, MI 49915, or visit its website at www.ironcountyhistoricalmuseum.org or via http://pointsnorthbooks.com/sites

Kingston Lake
Alger County

Paddling the lake

Although someone cannot turn back the clock to choose options not taken, sometimes choices that were taken can be turned into a campground. Kingston Plains, buried deep within the eastern part of Alger County, achieved notoriety for its lack of tree growth. At one time, it boasted one of the largest White Pine forests in the Midwest. The lumber trees were logged to nearly the very last one. The remains litter the plains, with fields of 125-year-old stumps marking the area like gravestones at Arlington. Nestled within all of this is Kingston Lake. In stark contrast, deeply wooded plains surround the area.

Located near the center of Pictured Rocks National Lakeshore, the region is not a part of that park but is run by the State of Michigan. County Road H-58, on which Kingston Lake State Forest Campground lies, used to be one of the roughest in the Upper Peninsula. But the road, also known as the Pictured Rocks Road, which runs between Munising and Grand Marais, has since been paved and now ranks as one of the smoothest in the state. Thus Kingston Lake is becoming more recognized and used.

Fortunately, the design of this campground couldn't be better. The main portion sits on a peninsula, and almost all of the 16 sites available are along the water, which offers convenience to paddlers. The lake supports fantastic fishing and provides a small boat launch.

As a boon for hikers, the Fox River Trail runs through Kingston Lake campground. Follow it 4 miles to the north, where it connects with Lake Su-

From top to bottom:
Back in the bayous
Campsite
Back water paddling
Female Mallard

perior and the main Pictured Rocks Trail. To the south, the trail runs 27 miles to Seney, but be careful on this, as it doesn't get as many hikers and in spots the trail can be difficult to follow. Be sure to have maps and a GPS.

Kingston Lake State Forest Campground supplies rustic simplicity, with no hookups of any kind; the water source is a hand pump. No cell-phone service reaches the area, which can be good or bad, depending on your perspective. Planners who designed the campground long ago originally intended the area for tents and small travel trailers. Today's RVs and huge trailers, more mobile home than trailer, struggle here. The sites are too small and the roadway tight and narrow. Most can barely inch around the curve at the end of the peninsula. As entertaining as that can be to watch, it puts a frowny face on most vacations.

My personal favorite reason for staying here is the wildlife, which thrives. Little coves and lagoons, features of Kingston Lake, provide nesting for a multitude of species. Loons, ducks, and herons can be seen and heard day and night, while a keen eye can spot beaver, muskrat, and otter. While paddling, I came across a turtle nesting ground. A mother loon with her babies paddled on the south side of the lake. Most of the wildlife here seem aware of the constant human presence of the park and are tolerant to a degree. I was able to get quite close to some of the animals for photography.

With Loon calls echoing across the water, Kingston Lake doesn't get more iconic Northwoods than that. It even comes with the occasional Lake Superior storm. Coyotes howl at the moon from time to time. Centrally located, Kingston Lake is within 30 miles of everything Pictured Rocks, Munising, and Grand Marais has to offer. For more information on Kingston Lake State Forest Campground (although I have to admit that my write-up is better than that on the site), go here: https://www.michigan.org/property/kingston-lake-state-forest-campground

or via http://pointsnorthbooks.com/sites

Lake Antoine
Dickinson County

Sitting next to Iron Mountain, Lake Antoine maintains the feel of an old fashioned community park.

We often look back on a world gone by with nostalgia and longing. The small-town lake with the beach and lifeguard haunts our memories. A bandstand on a summer evening, ice cream cones at the beach concession stand, the family barbecue, bike rides around the campground in circle after circle, the pastoral summers of the past—we see them in movies, but most are lost to time. Lake Antoine in Iron Mountain harkens back to those memories, charm and all.

Lake Antoine Park hasn't changed in 80 years; it could be a scene right out of an old movie. Its sparkling water and surrounding high bluffs create a UP flavor hard to resist.

Lake Antoine is a community gathering place for year-round local events such as boat races, snowmobile races, fishing tournaments, and Fourth of July fireworks. It is a regular destination for tourists and locals both.

Situated on the north east side of the lake on Lake Antoine Road (and partially within Iron Mountain city limits), it runs directly off U.S. Route 2. Nearly one hundred sites spread throughout tall pines. The evening brings a view of daily sunsets from the sandy shoreline. Waterfowl nest and flock here, so wildlife proliferates.

Campsites range from modern to primitive. Costs are small with extra for water and electric hookups. Bathrooms have hot and cold running water with showers.

Lake Antoine Park, open from May to September, is a wonderful family experience, with a playground and a beach with a lifeguard. A concession stand conducts business during summer months. A large pavilion provides excellent coverage for get-togethers and family reunions. Weather won't spoil summertime here.

A public boat launch for small to midsize boats provides access to the fairly large lake that can accommodate most pleasure boats. The lake is excellent fishing for pan fish, walleye, and pike. Fishing tournaments frequent the yearly schedule. Contact the local Chamber of Commerce about specific dates and events.

Several other small fishing areas are within a short driving distance. A couple of small lakes, as well as the Menominee River, are large enough to accommodate small craft for excellent deep-river fishing.

If sightseeing is your passion, fear not. Relics of a rich history abound in Iron Mountain. You can see remnants of the old mines and the businesses associated with them around the local countryside. This is carried on through town where time has been spent in restoring and refurbishing local historic buildings. The turn of the century feel permeates the town, as Iron Mountain has prioritized restoring and refurbishing local historic buildings. Historical

The tall pines within the park at Lake Antoine. (top)
Pileated Woodpecker (bottom)

museums help to understand the area and the origins of Iron Mountain.

The Cornish Pump and Mining Museum is a must-see for understanding the local heritage, while the World War II Glider and Military Museum reflects the military heritage of Dickinson County. Both museums are at the same location, two blocks from US 2. For the

Fishing dock

rest of the local history, the Menominee Range Historical Museum, also at the same location, highlights the daily life of the early residents.

Viewing the countless bats that come out of the "bat cave" should be on your to-do list. The cave, the former Millie Mine, is a major habitat for bats. In the evening they come out in great flocks as they venture out to consume insects by the tons.

Small streams appear all around the area; each has good to excellent trout possibilities for the stream fisherman.

The Jim and Ida Goulette Senior Citizen Park, on the north side of the lake, sits in a small island/peninsula covered with tall pines. The park welcomes those who need a spot for a picnic or a site to enjoy the scenery, but it isn't for camping. The big attraction of Goulette Park is for handicapped fishermen. A fishing platform stretches out into the lake, providing comfortable fishing opportunities for those who have a hard time getting around the traditional sites. This little park is one of the more relaxing locations in the Iron Mountain area. I suggest stopping and enjoying it even if for a few minutes.

Less than 2 miles from Lake Antoine Park is the Fumee Lake Natural Area, which has abundant hiking trails, ranked from novice to expert, and plenty of wildflowers and wildlife. The trails range from less than a mile to nearly 5 miles. Two former mine sites, the Indiana and the Illinois, are included in one of the trails, though the Indiana is right near a parking area.

With the lake situated virtually inside the city limits, you will have no problem finding supplies locally for camping or any of the local recreation.

In the winter, the park itself is closed, but events still occur at Lake Antoine, like snowmobile races and fishing derbies. Like most UP areas now, snowmobile trails are abundant. Winter sports abound in this area, such as skiing, from downhill to cross-country. The Pine Mountain Ski Jumping tournament, always a popular event, takes place in the winter.

Are small-town community parks a thing of the past? Not in Iron Mountain. It's a place to rediscover local traditions and the pure fun of being at the lake.

For more information, contact Iron Mountain Chamber of Commerce at www.cityofironmountain.com or via http://pointsnorthbooks.com/sites

Lake Gogebic
Ontonagon County

Lake Gogebic is nearly 20 miles long, is situated in two counties and sits in both the Eastern and Central time zones.

The waters sparkle as the long lake snakes off into the horizon. Lake Gogebic, in the western end of the Upper Peninsula, is the U.P.'s largest inland lake, large enough that it lies in two counties (Ontonagon and Gogebic) and two time zones. The residents of the area want you to come and enjoy it.

Lake Gogebic has earned a reputation for being one of the outdoor sporting hot spots of the UP. It also provides fine locations for any outdoor recreational activity.

Like most places in the Upper Peninsula, Bergland Township, located next to Lake Gogebic, has a rich history. To the north was copper mining, while to the south was iron mines. Logging surrounded Gogebic itself. Just to the east in a place called Matchwood, the company Blue Diamond Matches began. The Ontonagon River runs out of the north end of Lake Gogebic and was dammed in the late 1800s. The wider lake today resulted from that project.

On the south end of Lake Gogebic, in the 1800s there were many early resorts on the shore. A regular stage coach ran between there and Iron Mountain. On August 26, 1889, the passengers were held up in what would be the last stage-

Bergland jailhouse (top)
Bergland Museum display (bottom)

with an innocent bystander who later died. It was believed that the passenger not Holzey killed the man. Holzey escaped and fled to Republic, Michigan where he checked into a hotel under an assumed name. The hotel manager recognized him and summoned the local sheriff who arrested Holzey the next morning as he was coming out. After 23 years in prison Holzey committed suicide in 1952. A sad end to an ill conceived life.

Since the 1800s, resorts have been a staple on Gogebic's shores. Lake Gogebic is known for its legendary fishing, though, surprisingly, not many people take advantage of it. Trophy walleye, perch, northern pike, and bass proliferate.

The 18-mile-long and mile-and-a-half-wide lake is surprisingly shallow for its size, with the maximum depth at 35 feet. High reed grass bays, lily-pad shallows, barren sand bottoms, lush seaweed beds, deep cold granite pits, and sandstone ridges offer a wide variety of fish habitat, which accounts for the high fish population. The maximum depth is thirty-five feet with a wide range of bottom structure provides opportunities for any species fisherman. If one method doesn't work, head out to another section of lake and try there. Going from one section to another is like being in a completely different lake.

The fantastic length of the lake also makes for some fantastic paddling for kayakers. With miles of lagoons, coves and inlets, paddlers can enjoy scenery and wildlife where ever they stay on Lake Gogebic.

Surrounding Gogebic are accommodations galore. No matter how you like to spend your getaways, a special place exists to suit your taste and budget. Three public parks line the lakeshore, one run by the state and two run by the county. They are nicely separated from

coach robbery east of the Mississippi! A masked man, calling himself "Black Bart" attempted to rob the passengers. This was not the "famous" Black Bart, but a small time hood by the name of Reimund Holzey who was desperately trying to change his luck. It didn't work. One of the passengers refused to get with the program, pulled a gun and tried to shoot Holzey. Holzey shot back. The passenger was shot along

The dam that creates the modern version of Lake Gogebic.

each other, one on the north end, the next in the center, and the last located at the south, with all on the west side of the lake and all reasonably well sheltered from bad weather. The public parks are very well kept, have ample space, and are fully equipped with all of the hook-ups. The proximity gives the camper a choice of where on the lake to stay, or, if the camper is unhappy with one facility, he or she can move to another without leaving the area. The parks have launch facilities, as well as modern bathrooms and showers. Though these parks have quite a few regulars, a large portion of the campsites remain unused. The campgrounds also have playgrounds and beaches for the youngsters.

Motels and resorts have sprung up all around the lake and range from budget to private luxury. Many of the motels and resorts provide boat and equipment rentals as well as private guide services. The Gogebic Lodge, the Timbers Resort, and the Root Cellar Resort all provide fishing and hunting guides, which can be advantageous if you are unfamiliar with the area or have limited time. Reservations are suggested to enable these resorts to prepare the experience you are looking for.

Some excellent restaurants and pubs occupy the neighborhood; JW's BBQ & Brew and the Hoop N Holler Tavern are both excellent food stops. Antonio's Restaurant has good family cooking, including breakfasts, daily specials, and fresh baked goods.

The Gogebic Lodge has accommodations for large parties and has live entertainment. Its docking facilities are large enough to tie up a seaplane, though it doesn't provide aviation fuel. Dock gas pumps for boats are available, however.

Many smaller resorts and motels have their own merits and at lower cost. If you investigate before arriving, you can certainly find someplace to provide exactly what you're looking for. Contacting the Lake Gogebic Area Chamber of

Bergland old town along tracks

Commerce will save hit-or-miss choices as well.

Though fishing is the area's claim to fame, the hunting ranks among the best. Logging over the years has left many tracts open, which have consistently increased the white-tailed deer and ruffed grouse populations. Other than locals, few people come in to hunt the area. Good habitat, the lack of fishing pressure and several years of mild winters have given the Gogebic area an overwhelming game increase.

This portion of the U.P. boasts the densest deer population, with the exception of the Menominee/Delta farmlands. More important, State and Ottawa National Forest land surrounds the Lake Gogebic. Yes, that means an abundance of open public lands. Maps from the U.S. Forest Service and State of Michigan Department of Natural Resources show the specifics.

Lake Gogebic, and dozens of small isolated but accessible lakes provide fantastic photography and are fun to explore. Ducks, geese, and water birds of all kinds use the area as a major nesting ground and migratory stop. The isolated bays and inlets, surrounding wetlands, and lakes provide more than adequate shelter and isolation for even the shyest of species. A beneficiary is, of course, the Gogebic visitor.

Local residents have organized off-road vehicle and snowmobile clubs that work tirelessly to create trails. Many have been completed and complement the wonderful sights Gogebic offers, such as high bluff overlooks and local waterfalls. Several trails utilize old railroad grades, which take the user to regions only accessible that way. They hit other sites, such as ghost towns and old mines. The groups use all available trails and as a result are creating one of the most extensive trail systems in the U.P.

The clubs frequently host events; organized runs and outings are held year round. Currently, snowmobiling brings in more visitors to the area than anything else. The area Chamber owns a trail groomer for snowmobilers, which operates continuously all winter, insuring top quality trail conditions.

The Gogebic area is suited for hiking or backpacking. Several local hiking trails extend through the region, and

Public Access Bergland

the North Country Trail (N.C.T.) runs through the north side. The N.C.T., a hiker's route, runs from New York to the Dakotas and is designed to hit as many scenic wonders as possible.

In the Gogebic area, that aspect is particularly prominent. The N.C.T. extends through the Trap Hills, part of the Gogebic range of mountains. The trail takes the hiker up and over escarpments and ridges that provide spectacular views. The U.S. Forest Service designated the region a special interest area due to its dramatic beauty and ruggedness. The Trap Hills are not for the faint of heart.

Paddling in the southern section of the lake can bring some surprises. Wide river outlets at the south end of Gogebic meander into the wilderness. Paddling further downstream will lead to waterfalls, accessible only by canoe. It is best to study these routes before paddling, especially by those trying to reach the Nelson Canyon Falls. A few miles to the south, in the Watersmeet area, is the Sylvania Wilderness Tract, famous for its water-connected lakes and canoe trails. Small, isolated bodies of water dot the entire southern portion of Gogebic County; they have many passable water connections that aren't a part of Sylvania Wilderness, a protected area west of Watersmeet Township. It has been compared frequently to Boundary Water, a canoe wilderness area in Minnesota.

Surprisingly, the Gogebic area isn't overrun with visitors. It is easy to get to from all directions, particularly for residents in Wisconsin and Minnesota. M-28 and U.S. Route 2 both route by Gogebic. With all of the opportunities that are offered here, Lake Gogebic is a good time waiting to happen, no matter what you like to do. After your first visit, it will become a permanent destination for you and your family. Investigate it—you'll be impressed. For more information go to the region's website at www.lakegogebicarea.com.

Little Girls Point Gogebic County

North of Ironwood is a place steeped in legend and mystery. A rugged and sandy section of the Lake Superior shoreline, it is isolated and serene, lonely and mystic. It should have a legend.

The legend goes as follows: A daughter of a Chippewa hunter named Leelanau loved to look out over Lake Superior and canoe along the shoreline to places she found enjoyable. One of her favorites was Little Girl's Point, which could be seen from her home, what is now known as the Escarpment Trail in Porcupine Mountains Wilderness State Park. She was repeatedly told never to go there because it was a sacred place haunted by spirits—Puk Wadginees or "the little men of the wood." She didn't heed the warnings, and on the day of her wedding she disappeared there. A thorough torchlight search of the woods revealed nothing, and no trace of her was ever found.

Fishermen claimed to see a man and a woman walking the beach. The pair disappeared upon attempts to approach them. This, of course, has only fueled the legend's life.

Another story is that the Incas, or Aztecs, had made their way north, fleeing the Spanish and carrying a huge treasure of gold. They came up the Mississippi and into Lake Superior, eventually

Little Girls Point is a small Lake Superior village that is isolated and peaceful. (top) This sign stands in the campground and gives an account of the legend of the "Little Girl." (bottom)

hiding their gold somewhere around Little Girls Point. One of the early residents of Little Girls Point, George Triplett, took this legend seriously.

Triplett began digging all around the Little Girls Point area, prospecting. Though the region had long been considered worthless for commercial mining, he dug one pit after another, some 80 to 100 feet deep. Triplett found some silver and copper and hinted at other things.

He was even able to use the story of lost Native American treasure to get some investors. For years he dug, but if the lost treasure was there, he never found it.

To get to Little Girls Point, go north of Ironwood from U.S. Route 2, taking County Road 505. The drive is about 21 miles on blacktop highway. Just about the time you think you've gone too far, you're there.

Little Girls Point is an out of the way place, virtually unknown and rarely seen. The park there is seldom filled, which is too bad because Little Girls Point is a wonderful place to stay and enjoy.

A long stretch of beach has campsites right on the shoreline, 30 total. The main road is a lakeside drive, so any vehicle can access the campsites.

These campsites are an extension of one of the nicest little parks around. The park is well groomed and peaceful, carved out of a hardwood grove that provides an enjoyable atmosphere for the family. With the beach, a picnic area, and a playground, it makes the ideal place to spend summer hours.

Because a small community surrounds the solitude of Little Girls Point, a couple of small curio and trinket shops are on hand, including an excellent rock shop that sells and displays the local gems. A docking facility is behind the shop, dredged out of the mouth of Oman's Creek.

A public boat launch accesses this remote section of Superior, where fishing pressure is minimal. The river gets seasonal trout and salmon runs in the spring and fall, and a fisherman can do well.

To add to the mystique of the Native American legend, a few hundred yards into the woods reveals a lone gravesite. A small sign along the road marks the meandering trail to the resting place among tall trees. A simple square barrier is made of old cedar logs. Towering over the grave

A Lake Superior fog settles across the playground at the Little Girls Point campground. (top) My wife making use of the swing at Little Girls Point. Another legend says that this place will bring out the little girl in everyone, though that shouldn't be gender specific.

is an old totem pole, a sentinel for the one who made the spirit journey.

Little Girls Point has no store of any kind where a traveler can get food and drink, so when planning a trip here, make sure supplies are picked up in Ironwood.

A trip to Little Girls Point makes a beautiful and restful vacation stay. It is a perfect place for the whole family, and the stories of the area should prompt many hours of conversation and speculation. A Chippewa protection tome reflects the feel of the point: "Spirits of the green wood plume, shed around thy leaf perfume, such as spring from buds of gold which thy tiny hands unfold, Spirits hither, Spirits repair!" (The quote was taken from sign in park.) For more information on the park at Little Girl's Point go here: https://www.allstays.com/Campgrounds-details/21433.htm or via http://pointsnorthbooks.com/sites

Little Presque Isle
Marquette County

The moon rises over Little Presque Isle and Lake Superior located in Marquette County.

N orth of Marquette, in Michigan's Upper Peninsula, is a place for all seasons and things. Does that sound too good to be true? Nestled in the foothills of Lake Superior's Huron Mountains range, the Little Presque Isle Recreation Area has virtually everything that someone would want when going outdoors: backtrail hiking, fishing, hunting, cross-country skiing, snowmobiling, swimming, rock climbing, or simply a treat for the senses. A quick drive 5 miles north of Marquette on County Road 550 will get you there. The area has always been something of a secret but has been well known to local residents for years.

The Michigan State Department of Natural Resources developed the section for recreational activities and spent well over a quarter of a million dollars completing it. Trails are marked and kept, while the streams and lake is already well stocked. Because of the region's diversity, visitors can spend countless hours doing a variety of activities year round.

Outdoor activities can revolve around five basic locations that make up the area: Sugarloaf Mountain, Hogsback

Mountain, Wetmore Landing, Little Presque Isle, and Harlow Lake. Not any of them cost more than the time and effort it takes to enjoy them.

Sugarloaf Mountain

The well-marked entry to the mountain is located not quite 4 miles north of Marquette. The trail to the top of the mountain is well kept and similarly well marked. Where the going gets steep, hand-railed stairways make climbing easy and reasonably pleasant. Benches are placed for an occasional breather if the need arises. Though a nice climb during summer, the hike in winter has extra treats on the way up. Coming out of the rock outcroppings are small running springs or water seepages that run constantly; in the freezing weather, wonderful and sometimes colored icicle formations continually grow. Arriving at the summit reveals miles of view of Lake Superior, Marquette, Little Presque Isle, and all of the surrounding area, including that of nearby Hogsback Mountain.

Hogsback Mountain

The trail for Hogsback Mountain is 1 mile north of Sugarloaf's parking lot and on the opposite side of the road. It is marked as the Harlow Lake Trail but also serves as Hogback's. The walk is lengthy and at times strenuous, with no climbing aid, necessitating the hiker to be in reasonably good physical shape. The trail starts out as an old two-rut trail before it splits as it follows along an abandoned railroad grade. Follow the railroad grade to the left. If you go to the right, you would be on the Harlow Lake Trail, an excellent hiking and skiing trail. Straight ahead trails wander into the woods in a maze; getting lost is a good possibility for those unfamiliar with the trails. But if you can learn them, a lifetime of exploring by skiing,

Harlow Creek is great for fishing at the Little Presque Isle Recreation Area. (top) Hogsback Mountain stands majestically over Harlow Lake at the Little Presque Isle Recreation Area. (middle) In the winter an ice bridge connects Little Presque Isle with the mainland. (bottom)

hiking, or snowmobiling is possible. Follow the trail to the left for a couple of hundred yards until a footpath runs into the woods to the right. Large painted spots on the trees mark the trail. Follow the mark, and the summit is about 30 minutes away. The true enjoyment of this trail comes from traveling through a deep mix of hardwood and pine decorated by massive rock outcrops, in addition to the wildlife frequently seen on the trail. Another attraction of this walk is solitude; whereas Sugarloaf has a good deal of traffic on it, other hikers on Hogsback are few and far between—or none at all. The different position and higher altitude yield views of Harlow Lake and some other surrounding wetlands that cannot be seen from Sugarloaf. The hike is about 4 miles roundtrip and well worth it.

Wetmore Landing

The entrance to Wetmore Landing lies directly across the road from that of Hogsback. The landing is a cove with one of the finest sheltered beaches around, a pocket of pleasure surrounded by rock and cliffs. The cliffs are similar to those that make up Pictured Rocks National Lakeshore but on a smaller scale.

Hiking trails run from here to Sugarloaf, which affords some spectacular shoreline scenery. Snowshoeing the trail in the winter is like entering another world. Hanging snow, ice-covered shrubs and trees from splashing water of waves crashing, dozens of hanging-ice formations from free-flowing water and springs, and the shoreline heavily sheltered from prevailing winds all makes for unique winter snowshoeing.

In the other direction, a trail runs to Little Presque Isle. This will take you up and onto the cliffs that are almost copies to those that make up Pictured Rocks, revealing wonderful views of Lake Superior and the incredible shoreline. Wetmore Landing is also one of the best swimming and picnic spots available, especially because of its sheltered nature.

Little Presque Isle

The entrance to Little Presque Isle is 1.2 miles north of Wetmore Landing on the same side of the road, just a few feet south of Harlow Creek. The isle, favored by the locals, has an extensive beach and stands offshore; a shallow sand bar con-

nects it to the mainland. In the summer, visitors can wade to the island through Lake Superior, and in winter, a wide ice bridge connects to Little Presque Isle. Many come here to camp or view the rock formations that make up a good portion of the island and the shoreline.

In the winter, after a good east-northeast storm, ice encases Little Presque Isle and the surrounding shoreline. The rare scene lends itself to photography, excellent viewing when skiing or snowshoeing, or simply a winter walk. Picnickers should always get supplies before they leave Marquette because no stores are along the road.

Harlow Lake

Harlow Lake's entrance lies directly across County Road 550 from Little Presque Isle. With Hogsback Mountain always standing over the lake in the distance, the scenery is beautiful. Many diverse species of wildlife, including those rare and endangered, live here. The lake holds many different kinds of fish, including pan fish and pike; three fast-moving cold-water streams containing brook and rainbow trout feed the lake. Eagles commonly hunt the lake.

This place is already a playground for skiers, hikers, snowmobilers (miles of trails branch off from Harlow Lake), fishermen (including ice fishers), boaters, canoers, and those relaxing in the pines or on one of the immense granite rocks exposed on the lake. The area offers rustic campsites and public access for boats—but small craft only. One-room, fully equipped cabins can be rented by contacting the Marquette, Michigan, D.N.R. office.

If a trip to Michigan's Upper Peninsula is in the plans, then the Little Presque Isle Recreation Area should be a part of them. More info at http://points-northbooks.com/sites

Manistique Lakes and Curtis Schoolcraft County

There are several streams that feed the waters of South Manistique Lake and they can be fun to kayak into. The mouth of one can be seen in the middle left of the picture.

What has over 15 thousand acres of water and over 30 resorts? That's Curtis, Michigan, located in Michigan's eastern central Upper Peninsula. Sandwiched between North and South Manistique Lakes, the village is the unlikeliest of destinations, yet no vacation there is boring. With small shops galore and two large lakes, Curtis and the Manistique Lakes have something for everyone.

For year-round fun there is no place like the Curtis area. Three lakes, miles of trails, and two public campgrounds make this a place that can be enjoyed by anyone, anytime.

Manistique Lakes is one of the UP's best-kept secrets. Located between U.S. Route 2 and M-28, a traveler doesn't accidentally go through it. Consequently, it has always been a place for those in the know.

The local chamber of commerce has spent many years making this a haven for recreation. Ongoing fishing contests happen throughout the year, snowmobile and ORV trails are laid out for miles, and the public lands surround the place. Fishing and hunting is some of the finest, and the area boasts one of the largest deer herds.

The two public campgrounds are on North Manistique Lake and South

South Manistique Lake campsite (top)
South Manistique Lake duck family (middle)
Boat launch at the Luce County Park on North
Manistique Lake. (bottom)

picnic area, unsupervised beach, volleyball net, and swing set for the kids.

The lake is known for warm-water fish, such as traditional freshwater species, particularly walleye, but not trout, which is a cold-water fish. Public access can accommodate small boats; in the winter, fishermen can use the access for ice fishing.

Easy to find, the campground is located on the south side of the lake in the town of Helmer. Roads from Germfask and McMillan both lead to the park. County Road 98 comes in from M-77 at Germfask and swings north to M-28 east of McMillan. The campground costs only a few dollars a night.

Big Manistique Lake

Big Manistique Lake covers twice the area of the other two. No state or public-run campground is on the lake, but private ones are. Public accesses are available for boats, and the lake is a small jaunt from either campground.

The lake too has excellent fishing, with a reputation for walleye and pan fish.

South Manistique Lake

The state forest campground resides near this lake. Costing a few dollars a night, the campground runs according to an honor system but is checked periodically. A list shows fined campers who didn't register and pay. Signs mark well the route to the campground located off South Curtis Road. As with the campground on North Manistique Lake, the facilities here are primitive.

Thirty sites populate the campground, which a small boat access. An access site for bigger boats is up the road back toward Curtis. I recommend that one over the one at the campground unless you are paddling.

Manistique Lake. The rest on the lake are private, though most are nice and have reasonable fees. As with so many of the Upper Peninsula state forest campgrounds, places are always available. The campgrounds are not open year round, but they stay open while accessible.

North Manistique Lake

Luce County runs the campground on North Manistique Lake. Though small, it has 30 sites. The campground supplies electricity but no other amenities. The park is well groomed, with a

Camping at Luce County Park is a bit different than camping at South Manistique.

Half the sites are along the shoreline, and the others are set back in the woods.

No beach is located here. The shore is weedy, and the woods goes to the water's edge. The bottom of the water is sandy. A small nature trail allows for a nice hike. The park is quiet, secluded, and bare bones.

Numerous private resorts surround all three lakes, with beaches and cabins. Each lake has bed and breakfasts located on them; one of the best is Chamberlin's Ole Forest Inn, which serves some of the finest food in the Upper Peninsula. None of these places is outrageously priced, and most are open all year.

Curtis, which hosts the World Champion Turtle Races in the summer, boasts restaurants, stores, and small shops. The Fish and Hunt Shop has everything for those who enjoy the outdoors, and, more important, it repairs all toys. It even rents snowmobiles in the winter.

A stop by the Erickson Art Center in Curtis can be very rewarding. The displays change regularly and showcase area artists who will surprise and amaze.

Surrounding area streams provide trout fishing and paddling. The Seney National Wildlife Refuge, only 20 miles away, provides amazing wildlife-viewing opportunities of rare and endangered species. The Black Creek Flooding Area, part of Curtis, brings in ducks and geese for the hunters.

During the winter, nothing slows down. Curtis grooms 50 miles of snowmobile trails and several established cross-country ski trails. Of course, ice fishing is a major pastime. The lakes are relatively shallow and freeze early and safely. Curtis even holds dog-sled races.

This area is geared for nothing but fun. No matter what activities you enjoy, the Manistique Lakes area has someplace for you to do them. A visit here can't help but be quiet and relaxing. For more information on places, prices, and accommodations, contact Manistique Lakes Area Tourism Bureau, P.O. Box 8-A, Curtis, MI 49820, or call the Curtis Area Chamber of Commerce at 906-586-3700. Check out its website at www.curtischamber.com or via http://pointsnorthbooks.com/sites.

McCormick Wilderness Tract Marquette County

•● ⬛ ●•

The tall granite bluffs stand like monuments amid thriving virgin pine and ancient hardwoods. Out of these cliffs flow countless springs that feed and nurture streams or lakes nestled within the valleys between them. Wildlife, occasionally appearing out of curiosity, abounds throughout the area. This wilderness is a different world, remote and solitary, a world of escape for a rich and famous man, Cyrus H. McCormick, the inventor who made his fortune mechanizing farming.

The McCormick Tract contains over 17 thousand acres of absolute wilderness, acquired by its namesake after the logging rush of the early 1900s. Realizing many stands of virgin pine and hardwoods remained in the area, McCormick purchased this vast acreage containing lakes, mountains, and streams, some of the most aesthetically pleasurable in the Upper Peninsula. He deeply loved this land, refusing any type of environmental exploitation. He searched the property, exploring until he discovered the place eventually named White Deer Lake. McCormick chose the site for a cluster of log and stone cabins, a grand camp fit for a man of his stature. This became his private and personal playground, remaining in the family until 1969, when the family donated it to the U.S. Forest Service.

Until 1987, the U.S.F.S. used the area for research in forest ecology, allowing primitive recreation only—hiking and skiing, but not overnight camping. But today, due to a bill passed in the legislature designating wilderness areas, camping is allowed, and the area can be more fully experienced. Motorized vehicles, however, are not permitted.

Located 3 miles west of Champion, or 1 mile west of Van Riper State Park off U.S. Route 41, the tract is on County Road 607, also known as the Peshekee Grade Road. Travel 8 miles north after leaving U.S. Route 41 until you spot a dirt turnoff to the right; take that turnoff, which ends after approximately 100 feet. A gated bridge spans the beautiful

Peshekee River, marking the beginning of the hiking trail leading into the tract.

Forest, wetlands, and wildlife are evident along the trail, which meanders between rock bluffs abundant with fresh flowing springs. Located only about 5 miles from the moose lift release area the McCormick Tract is the location of the best chance in the U.P. of a hiker spotting one of these rarely seen creatures.

After about 3 miles, the trail ends at White Deer Lake, where McCormick's showcase camp once stood. A vast clearing provides an ideal campsite. Portaging a canoe, raft, or small boat can bring unexpected pleasure because miles of navigable waterways begin here. Headwaters of several large rivers, including the Yellow Dog and Dead Rivers, are located at White Deer Lake.

Old hiking trails made by the McCormick family can still be found and used. Several scenic overlooks reveal spectacular views of the distant Huron Mountains and long, wide valleys.

An area for all seasons, the wilderness unveils radical differences from one season to the next. Winter provides cross-country skiing and snowshoeing filled with rare solitude. Long icicles, fed by the springs, decorate the bluffs. Dense forest offers protection from the winds.

Springtime, the season of awakening and rebirth, is more evident in this wilderness, teeming with color and life. An ideal prescription for cabin fever, a day hike can cleanse the soul of winter stagnation while loosening dormant muscles.

During the heat of summer, the tract offers good fishing and a berry-lined trail. The thick, shaded forest and cool rock outcropping combine to make heat more tolerable. But summer

Cyrus McCormick portrait (left page)
Birch Cabin (for Ladies) (top)
Chimney Cabin (demolished by Army Corps of Engineers) (bottom)

brings bugs—nets and repellent are not only recommended but required.

The highlight is autumn; with the rare old hardwoods mixed with the pines, the visitor experiences gratitude for making the trip. The view from the bluffs is unsurpassed, the air cool, the insects gone.

Fishing and hunting are allowed in the tract, but deer are scarce, and this is moose country—the hunter must be sure before taking aim. Shooting moose is illegal. Many species of fish inhabit the lakes throughout the tract.

A lifetime of exploring awaits the visitor in this vast section of the national forest. The McCormick Tract can get into the blood and require regular visits. The question never arises of why the McCormicks chose this area for their private playground. There's nothing like it. More info at http://pointsnorthbooks.com/sites

McLain State Park
Houghton County

A rainbow over the Keweenaw Peninsula dazzles campers at McLain State Park after a storm moves through.

The waves of Lake Superior wash the pebble and sand Upper Peninsula beach. The light but ever-present Keweenaw Peninsula breeze adds an evening cool. On the horizon, the sun verges on submerging in the icy waters. To the southwest, the Porcupine Mountains are washed in pink, orange, and red. McLain State Park provides a view of this sunset.

McLain State Park is the alternative to Fort Wilkins State Park at Copper Harbor. Situated halfway between Houghton and Calumet in the Keweenaw Peninsula on M-203, McLain Park has something for everyone.

The park's location makes it ideal for exploring the historical treasures of the Keweenaw. Calumet and the National Heritage Park is 8 miles away. Copper Harbor and Fort Wilkins, which is the longest drive, is only 30 miles, and in between are dozens of ghost towns and the magnificent mountains of the peninsula. The extraordinary drive is beyond compare and a way to avoid the summer crowds that invade Fort Wilkins State Park.

Portage Entry Light

A larger day area and better beach than at Fort Wilkins and rental cabins make this park a prime choice for spending time in the Keweenaw. McLain State Park opens year round as well. The roads aren't plowed, but camping is allowed, and park employees are there. The employees suggest snowshoeing to the cabins.

The four-bunk, one-room cabins and one eight-bunk cottage are set away from the drive-in sites and face the beach and the sunset. They are equipped with mattresses, table, woodstove, electricity, and running water. The cost is low (around $30 per day) compared to resort cabins and motel fees. The experience is more personal and unusual for a state park. Reservations are suggested, though of course walk-ins are welcome if a rental is open.

The park boasts more than one hundred campsites of all types, from RV sites to tent sites equipped with all hookups available if needed. The camps run parallel to the beach; none are far from it. A playground is next to the beach.

A small park store is open during the summer, and modern bathrooms with showers are available as well. A public access called Lily Pond exists for boat enthusiasts 2 miles toward Calumet.

Bear Lake, an elegant small inland waterway located across M-203 from the park with a trail leading to it from the park side, provides for good panfishing, Using live bait is suggested. The trail circumnavigates Bear Lake, and the lake's natural beauty makes the 2-mile circular hike worth every step. Lots of opportunities for photography pop up along the way.

The entire park is barrier free. Blacktopped and ramped access exists for every facet of the park. This really is a place for everyone.

McLain State Park is well-groomed, clean, and appealing to stay in. Few places like this are in Michigan and the sunset makes leaving here difficult. This is a fantastic Keweenaw vacation spot. More info at http://pointsnorth-books.com/sites

Monocle Lake
Chippewa County

Beach magic hour

Misty clouds cling to the high bluffs of Mission Hill on an early morning. The water on the lake is still and calm. Great Horned Owl cries—*hoo hoo wa hoo*—echo through the valley. Monocle Lake is otherwise quiet, but only hours before, in the night as the full moon rose, the barks and howls of coyotes mixed with the strange screaming sounds of herons, creating a cacophony in the darkness, fascinating while a touch unnerving.

The U.S. National Forest Service runs Monocle Lake Campground on a large tract of federal land north of Brimley, Michigan, and part of the Bay Mills Indi-an Community. Mission Hill, a long ridge that runs for several miles, buttresses the western side of the lake, affording Monocle Lake a picturesque beauty.

Sitting on the shore, I realize that generations of Native Americans have been here before me. This lake provided fish and game for the local tribe; tribal members harvested furs heavily as they did timber. Canoes plied the water, and beneath the shadow of Mission Hill, they still do. The region thrives on as it always did—the timbers grow tall and the lake provides fish and game. But now the canoes belong to the campers.

Tubing (top)
Mission Hill (bottom left)
Residence (bottom right)

Some private residences adorn the lakeside, as Monocle Lake is situated near the local communities. Natural habitat and deep forest surrounds most of the lake, so wildlife abounds here. For photographers with patience and ambition, the area can be highly rewarding.

The area claims 40 rustic campsites; RVs and most but the largest trailers have no problems maneuvering and parking here. The facilities are pit toilets and a couple of water sources but no hookups.

The campground provides a boat ramp. The lake allows boats with motors, so it can be quite a playground. Naturally, fishing occurs. The sand bottom provides a nice beach, and the open lake is perfect for tubing. Small sailboats, kayaks, and canoes pass over Monocle Lake. ATVs seem the only restriction.

Only a couple miles separate Monocle Lake from the historical Iroquois Point Lighthouse and the beaches of Whitefish Bay. The Soo Locks and Tahquamenon Falls are only a few miles away. Whitefish Bay and the St. Mary's River are so close that campers on the lake can easily hear foghorns. Two casinos neighbor the campground: one, Bay Mills Resort and Casino, in Brimley and the King's Club Casino in Bay Mills. Some excellent restaurants are nearby; I recommend Wilcox Fish House and Restaurant, a few miles north and Pickles which is near the Bay Mills Resort and Casino.

Locals enjoy Monocle Lake, the campground, and the surrounding area; after visiting, you will quickly understand why. The whole family can play at the quiet little lake.

For more information go to this webpage: https://www.fs.usda.gov/recarea/hiawatha/recarea/?recid=13289, or call 906-428-5800 or visit http://pointsnorthbooks.com/sites

North Country Trail Entire UP

Sitting in front of three topographic maps, Jerry and I studied the elevation lines and color highlights for the best possible hiking and scenic route. "This looks like it could be good hiking—high rock, looks like there might be some bluffs here, stream gorge here." His finger ran from one point to another, moving from brown to green. "Let's go look." With that we scouted a route for the North Country Trail. That was 30 years ago when the North Country Trail project materialized in the Upper Peninsula.

This book has many references to the North Country Trail (N.C.T.), which begins in Port Henry, New York, and runs through Pennsylvania, Ohio, Michigan, Wisconsin, and Minnesota, before ending at Lake Sakakawea in North Dakota. The 3,340-mile trail winds its way through a series of the finest natural and historic areas in the northern tier of the Midwest. Michigan has the longest portion of any single state, and the Upper Peninsula section is breathtaking.

Running from St. Ignace to Ironwood, it travels through the most awe-inspiring sights the U.P. has. Of course, it winds through traditional areas, such as Tahquamenon, Pictured Rocks, and the Porcupine Mountains, but it also goes through sections previously inaccessible.

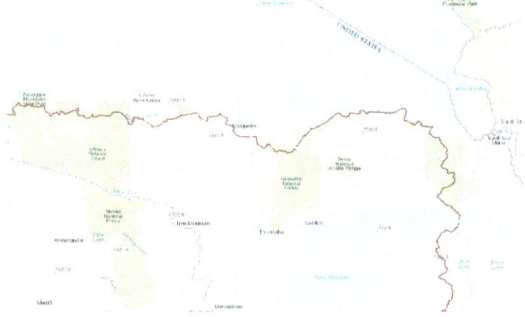

Upper Peninsula map of the North Country Trail.

The trail meanders through sections of Michigan's truest wilderness, taking the hiker miles away from any activity. The U.P. section of the N.C.T. is the most travelled section of the entire trail.

The North Country Trail Hikers Chapter diligently and steadily works throughout the year to maintain the trail. Doing so isn't easy; the logistics of building steps, bridges, and stairs is difficult when virtually all supplies and equipment must be carried into the sites by hand. When dealing with some of these deep wilderness areas, the problems sometimes seem insurmountable, but with teamwork and brainstorming chapter members manage to accomplish what sometimes seems impossible. They thrive on being outdoors and go into the wilderness hacking and slashing and tagging, keeping the trail marked and clear, battling the unending onslaught nature provides through downed trees and flooded streams.

Although the U.P.'s North Country Trail shows off many of the major and expansive sights, it leads to countless small and personal places too. The tumbling brooks, the quiet grottos, the deep undisturbed forests all make up the soul of this trail—places like Rock River Canyon, Sturgeon River Gorge Wilderness, and Trap Hills Escarpment.

The North Country Trail's original idea came from a plan the U.S. Forest Service proposed in the mid-60s. The initial design tried to incorporate as many previously established trails as possible. The trail route was established through forest lands first so some sections would be immediately in place for preferred locations. The U.S. Park Service was asked to give its recommendations. Next, the individual states linked their trail systems in, which is why the trail meanders frequently. Still, vast gaps came in between sections. Connecting the trail through the private lands in between public lands was a mammoth project.

Private volunteer trail organizations and individuals are responsible for most if not all trail development work. Four chapters of the North Country Trail Association are in the Upper Peninsula, with each responsible for a large section of the trail. They put on organized hikes that are also trail-marking and grooming treks.

The N.C.T. hikers chapters have been instrumental in running the trail through some of the most formidable and wild areas that weren't originally proposed for it. Places like the McCormick Tract, Little Presque Isle Recreation Area, Craig Lake State Park, Wildcat Canyon, and the Donnelley Wilderness Tract would never have

Volunteers

been considered if it weren't for the tenacity of these local chapters. The N.C.T. has several hundred members U.P.-wide.

Help occasionally comes from volunteer groups. Recently a Youth Corps group helped with some bridge building. Scout troops and summer youth groups often make trail projects part of their summer. The Northern Michigan University hiking class had a trail-building excursion.

Nearly every week, the chapters hold public hikes somewhere along the trail. It gets hikers out to see sections of the trail, showcases areas, and publicizes the chapters and the trail.

If you are interested in more information on the North Country Trail in the UP, write North Country Trail Association, 229 E. Main St., Lowell, MI 49331. Its website is very informative and includes downloadable maps: www.northcountrytrail.org.

Whether you plan a day hike or backpacking for any length of time, sections of the trail will suit your skills. No motorized vehicles are allowed on the trail at any time. More info at http://points-northbooks.com/sites

Old Victoria
Ontonagon County

Some of the old cabins being restored at Old Victoria.

It is a taste of homestead Upper Peninsula. Old Victoria, a ghost town from the copper boom, shows what life was like homesteading the U.P. Though some of the site has been destroyed or collapsed over the years, Old Victoria has many of its original homesteads still standing. Thanks to the efforts of a local group called the Society for the Restoration of Old Victoria, many of the buildings have been restored and refurnished in their original condition.

Old Victoria is thus one of the least known yet most interesting attractions the Upper Peninsula holds. The town was carved out of one of the harshest sections of the rugged UP landscape, situated at the top of a Michigan mountain part of the picturesque Ontonagon River Gorge, a part of the Gogebic Mineral Range. When visiting here, you get the feel for what it was like to struggle as a pioneer.

Old Victoria is 2 miles west of Rockland on Victoria Road. The drive in is steep and rocky, showing the formidable and rough landscape. Modern lifestyle makes relating to the settlers' survival predicament difficult. Furthermore, people of today would probably be dumbfounded over how they could make a living or, for some, make a fortune from the minerals that might be buried beneath.

The restored homesteads try to recreate that life. When you walk through them, you see how small and tight these homes were. The old and crude furniture and the ancient stoves show that comfort was nonexistent. Life was Spartan at best.

Old Victoria, part of the Keweenaw Heritage Trail, lists among the National Register of Historic Places. Like so many places in the U.P., Old Victoria's history is unique.

As early as the late 1700s, explorers dug into the hill that made up Victoria's landscape, looking for copper. Because of the harsh winter, they moved out after a few months of digging. But they didn't leave without finding what they were looking for—the hill was full of copper. At the bottom of their shaft was a one-ton piece of copper.

It laid there until the mid-1800s when the copper boom caused speculators to open mines all over the U.P., affecting Victoria. The early mining company invested hundreds of thousands of dollars on various mining ventures throughout the early years, without any payoffs. Victoria, perched at the top of a mountain, presented many problems difficult to overcome. The solutions to these problems gave Victoria its unique place in history.

The area was not going to make getting at the copper easy. From the start, mining attempts were plagued with problems. A forest fire destroyed all the buildings Victoria Mining Company had erected. Its stamp mill (a mill for crushing ore for further extraction) was destroyed, and a new one was built in a clearing along the Ontonagon River to prevent fire danger, only to have it swept away by a spring flood.

So much time was spent overcoming natural obstacles that no mining was done. The company even erected a giant windmill to pump water out of the mine and into the stamp mill. The Vic-

Reenactor (top)
Boy and accordian (middle)
Victoria Mine site (bottom)

toria Mining Company erected a sawmill to create timbers for shaft supports and used wood to fire the steam boilers, but, because of the forest fire, wood was scarce. So it had to find an alternative.

The company tried coal, but the grade was so steep from Rockland that a rail-

Victoria Dam

road was virtually out of the question. The Ontonagon River wasn't bridged, so a ferry had to be utilized, which raised the price of coal from $2.50 a ton to $8.00 just because of the 4-mile journey. At the turn of the century, the mine still made no money. Something had to be done.

That something came in the form of a device called the Taylor Hydraulic Air Compressor. It worked by dropping water from the river nearly four hundred feet into the ground through three intake shafts. Large amounts of air were introduced into the water through a special apparatus containing numerous small tubes located over each intake. The countless bubbles were then released in the air chamber cut from solid rock. The air was trapped by water at both the intake and the outlet and by the solid rock of the chamber itself. The air main then bled off the compressed air from near the top of the air chamber.

Because the compressor worked solely off the river's water, the compressed air was icy cold. It created a strange sight. Icicles would hang from the exhaust valves, and the operators had to bundle in heavy coats on hot summer days, working around the frost-covered machines. Icicles would form dozens of feet high surrounding a blow-off pipe that sprayed water and air into the sky.

It was a bizarre sight that became known as the Victoria Geyser. Local residents recall their ancestors telling them about the geyser. The compressor still exists to this day, and an effort to restore it is underway. Some believe it is still in working order.

Because of the compressor, suddenly the mine had no fuel costs. For the first time, the mine became profitable.

A dam was built to direct the water into the compressor, which also still stands. The town grew and eventually thrived, becoming a company town— with the company owning the houses. At the end of World War I, copper prices fell, and the town began its slide into a memory.

The town eventually fell to ruin, and plans were announced to burn the ruins. Some area residents would hear nothing of that. They formed a group

Restored log cabin

called the Society for the Restoration of Old Victoria and asked that the historic homes be spared. The society has made its goal the complete restoration of the lower log locations and the marking out of the old mining building locations at the mine site. The society created hiking trails, has maintained a picnic area, and opened to the public at no charge the old homes that are undergoing restoration or have been restored. All who come to Victoria can see a bit of the lives of those pioneer miners who lived there so long ago.

Old Victoria is believed to be the oldest log-cabin village in its original location in the United States. In recent years, a history class from one of the area schools has conducted a heritage project at Old Victoria. School children actually took residence in the village, living the lives of the pioneers, thereby learning about the past through experience.

Restoration is carried out by means of donations and fund-raising activities conducted by the society. Some of these are geared towards the general public and can really enhance a visit to Old Victoria. Log Cabin Day, which happens in mid-June, is one example. You can catch re-enactments and traditional cooking.

An annual craft fair held at Old Victoria is another such event; it features artists and crafts from all over. Held in August, the fair features traditionally cooked foods as well. The woodstove-cooked cinnamon rolls are gaining a reputation. Artists' tables are inexpensive.

Over the next year, the society hopes to start restoring two more buildings. Campsite creation is being considered as well; currently there is none.

The coming years promise to be ones of change in Old Victoria. Overwhelming scenery and special history make a visit worthwhile. The Society for the Restoration of Old Victoria is looking for any help it can get and encourages anyone to join. If you are interested in any information on Old Victoria, its activities, or events write: Old Victoria Historical Site, 25401 Victoria Dam Rd., Rockland, Michigan 49960 or visit http://pointsnorthbooks.com/sites.

Pentoga Park
Iron County

The drums pounded out a steady irresistible beat heard across the calm waters of the lake as long shadows moved and mingled with the tall pines and hardwoods. The huge ceremonial fire tinged everything around orange and yellow. The Ojibwa Native Americans danced in a circle around the fire. The humble village was silhouetted along the shore where birchbark canoes sat waiting to be taken out on the water for fishing. The ceremony honored one who passed on to the realm of the Great Spirit. The body had been put to rest in the burial ground on the far ridge. Occasionally mourning wails mingled with the drumbeats.

Pentoga Park rests on the former site of an Ojibwa village, a beautiful spot on one of Upper Michigan's nicest inland lakes, Chicagon Lake. The Native Americans frequently displayed impeccable taste on where they located their homes. Pentoga Park is on Iron County Road 424, 5 miles southwest of Crystal Falls and can also be reached by traveling south from Iron River to Caspian and then south 8 miles. The directions are well marked, so the park is easy to find.

This is Iron County's finest park. It is well groomed, is very clean, and has everything you would want in a park. Regardless of your preference, you'll find

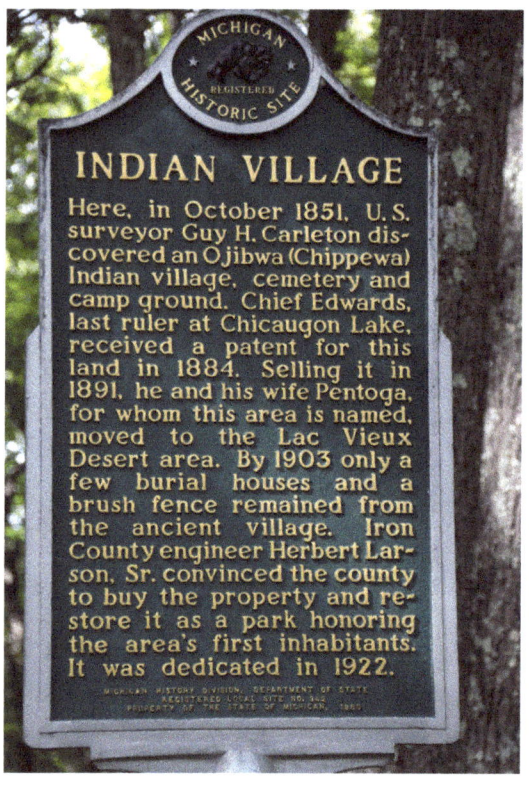

History marker

a place for it here. Exactly 104 campsites are in the park, equipped with all the hookups. All modern facilities such as showers and flush toilets are provided.

Facilities for all great warm weather activities are here. The lake brims with all traditional pan fish, from perch to pike. The park has a boat launching ramp, and the lake is large enough to provide good water skiing. A more-than-ample beach has a lifeguard on duty and comes equipped with the traditional playground toys every child enjoys.

A brick and stone pavilion sits on the beach. Half of it is a recreation and picnic area with a large stone fireplace. So you can still picnic in bad weather or have an evening get-together. The other half is a concession stand with traditional summer snacks from hot dogs to ice cream and everything in between.

Visitors notice the Native American heritage everywhere in the park. The ceremonial circle where the Native Americans danced and celebrated is marked and still intact, so the visitor can walk around it and envision its past. The site of the former the village is marked too. Former Native American trails are now used for hiking but still exist.

The burial ground, right on the edge of the campground, strikes the visitor more than any other Native American antiquity. Eerie yet fascinating, it will stimulate interest in Native American culture. The graves are unusual because of the custom this tribe had of building a shelter over each grave. At Pentoga, they are all intact, so visitors can note the differences and similarities in our cultures. Many of the questions that come up can be answered just up the road.

If you stay at the park, you should drive to the Iron County Museum in Caspian. Besides giving an excellent background on the area, the museum is unique in the state in that it constantly changes, adding on to itself. It has re-created an early mining town on a full scale. Original homesteads from the area have been moved on site along with a schoolhouse, a church, a railroad depot, and the house of a former songwriter. A modern building, constructed on the site, houses plentiful, in-depth, and interesting displays and artifacts.

Chicaugon Lake (top)
Native American burial ground. (bottom)

Dioramas of turn-of-the-century shops are packed with antiques, arranged for the patron to view authentic settlement surroundings. The museum exhibits local Native American artifacts, which give insight to the life, customs, and lore of the village at Pentoga.

Pentoga is actually the name of a Native American chief's wife. Literally translated, it means Bullhead. Whether she earned her name for her attitude or looks is unknown.

This is one of the most unusual parks I've ever seen and is also one of the cleanest and most accommodating. The family park will enhance the quality of your vacation. If you don't have a lot of time to spend, the campground is open for day use also. So no matter what type of schedule you're on, stopping here should be a part of it.

Staying here overnight is inexpensive, but fees have been subject to change. For current costs and further information contact the Crystal Falls Information Center, Junction US 2 and US 141, Crystal Falls, MI 49920, or call 906-875-4454 or visit http://pointsnorthbooks.com/sites.

Pequaming:
Ghost on the Water
Baraga County

A ghost makes its home in the Upper Peninsula, always present for all to see, only a shell of days gone by. The name of the ghost is Pequaming.

I saw it during one of those Lake Superior mornings when a low fog enshrouds and drapes everything, clouding but not obscuring. Through the morning mists, the ghost of Pequaming waited for another wayward traveler.

Pequaming is one of the largest still-standing ghost towns in the Upper Peninsula, a bygone piece of a very prosperous era in the history of Michigan. The town sits about 8 miles north of L'Anse on the shore of Lake Superior. Its pier, water tower, and Ford factory protrudes clearly into Keweenaw Bay.

To get to the old town, one merely has to go into L'Anse and drive the lakeshore road north. You can watch the ghost approaching through the majority of the drive. The road takes one directly into the former main street where Pequaming's remains dot the surrounding landscape: an old schoolhouse, general store, some of the homes, and the old Ford water tower and manufacturing plant. An old cemetery is also present and has weathered the years well.

Pequaming began, in its infancy, as a sawmill. It was founded in the late 1870s

Abandon boarding house (top)
Building and swing (bottom)

by Edward and Charles Hebard along with another man named H. C. Thurber, who stayed in the background. The initial investment into this venture was about $2 million, a massive amount for the time. The company purchased one hundred thousand surrounding acres and began producing 25 million feet of lumber and 25 million shingles annu-

Ghost buildings

ally. Mills and lumber camps scattered liberally throughout the woods needed nearly a thousand men.

The Hebard Company reared Pequaming into childhood by building company houses and a company owned general store. The workers rented homes and traded at the store; the bill was simply deducted from their wages. Pequaming was an example of a company town.

As the Hebard and Thurber mill grew, so did Pequaming. Tree-lined streets were established. The Hebards built a mansion for themselves, a 30-room southern-plantation style home on the lakeshore. Prosperity was making its mark.

The mill was the first and largest lumbering operation in the Lake Superior area, but it did something it didn't foresee. By 1910 it had exhausted almost all of the virgin pine timber in the area, slowing down operations to a trickle. Pequaming became desperately ill, and it might have died during childhood.

In 1920, a cure was found named Henry Ford. For his plants in Detroit, Ford decided to purchase approximately one million acres of land in the Upper Peninsula. Four hundred thousand of the acres purchased included the entire town of Pequaming and all of the holdings of the Hebard sawmill, including the nearly deserted lumber camps.

Ford believed in a certain amount of self-sufficiency, feeling that he should control all of the sources required for his industry, so he bought up large tracts of land to supply his plants with raw materials required in Detroit. Nearly all materials needed were found in abundance throughout the Upper Peninsula. A stone quarry located to the east of Pequaming and the remaining hardwoods untouched by the Hebards made Ford decide to make his largest single purchase in Upper Michigan there.

Henry Ford cured Pequaming so that it could become an adult, maturing as Ford's ideal model town. He revitalized and revamped the city with remodeled homes, a water tower (the one that can be seen today from nearly everywhere in the bay), and fire hydrants all through the town. Ford paid men

Old Ford factory

$6.00 for eight hours of work, which was a considerable amount, but strict rules had to be followed: no drinking, mandatory savings of a percentage of wages, and surveillance of their homes and general way of life.

Even the surrounding lumber camps were required to take on a new look and follow the rules much to the dismay of the rough and rowdy old lumberjacks. Buildings were erected in place of the tents, recreation halls with movies and radios were constructed, and in the mess halls the men ate balanced meals on china dishes. The camps even had electricity and running water.

In Pequaming, a hotel, more stores, three churches, a school, and railroads were all constructed according to Ford's personal specifications. Pequaming was a proud model to all of those around and Ford publicized it. He bought Hebard's mansion and resided in it during his revival of the town and made frequent stays after. Ford liked to keep a personal eye on how everything connected with his industry progressed.

Pequaming stayed prosperous and happy, a boon to the Ford family until the Depression of the 1930s. Like so much of the rest of America, the town suffered. The mills ran part time, but almost everyone was laid off. Again Pequaming fell ill.

With the outbreak of World War II, everything started back up, but this time work was done around the clock, six days a week. Even though the war gave it a boost of energy, Pequaming's illness never quite went away. It was terminal, this time with no cure.

The elimination of wood parts in automobiles after the war and the nearly depleted supply of hardwood killed Pequaming. The immaculate homes and lumber camps were subsequently abandoned. Pequaming passed away in 1948.

So next time you drive along the Keweenaw Bay, look and think about the ghost on the water, and maybe you'll see it waiting for the occasional wayfarer who imagines its once thriving life. More info at http://pointsnorthbooks.com/sites

Piers Gorge
Dickinson County

Rafters on the water braving the fury of Piers Gorge.

Piers Gorge, a section of the Menominee River, seems like it shouldn't be where it is. It should be someplace . . . wilder. It's a fast flowing section of the river that gives the Menominee its nickname, the U.P.'s Colorado River. The river has cut through the hills, creating high rock bluffs and, at different times of the year, violent white water. Dense woods encase all that, which creates rich, lush, and always impressive beauty.

To get there, drive 8 miles southeast of Iron Mountain on U.S. Route 2 into the town of Norway. Go due south on U.S. Route 8 less than 2 miles. A turnoff to the west is marked by a large sign. If you cross the bridge on U.S. 8 over the river, you just missed the turn. The road leading into the gorge starts out as blacktop but turns to dirt. Follow this to the end, at a circle turnaround. Park there.

A well-travelled and well-groomed hiking trail leads straight west into the woods. The trail is your access point. It follows the riverbank up and over bluffs, meandering through the thick woods, into aromatic cedar groves, through hardwoods and pines, past expansive views and lookouts over the river bed and surrounding bluffs and hills. Countless small feeder trails run down to the riverbed every few yards. The main hiking trail runs for approximately 2 miles along the river.

The four seasons bring radical changes, creating a seasonal diversity of beauty and methods to enjoy it. Spring generates high waters and wildly rushing rapids—and also kayakers and whitewater rafters. The hardy crew takes nature by the teeth just to see who comes out on top. They are wild! Their endeavors are quite something to see from the bluffs or riverbank. The scenes are a photographer's grab bag, when the river really looks like the Colorado, these people go through anything, and everything happens. Experienced kayakers or rafters with their own equipment gain their put-in and pull-out points on the path. Visitors may also enjoy wonderful spring backpacking and hiking on the path.

In summer, the waters recede drastically so that canoeing and fishing are possible. The river changes character, making visiting here a relaxing experience. Hiking and backpacking is moderate to easy so almost anyone can partake of the gorge's sights. From the circle where you park, the gorge is only a 10-15 minute walk in.

Fall has to be experienced to be believed. The high hills are an assault of color, with virtually every species of native hardwoods and pine mixed into the cover. Viewing it either by canoe or hiking is the way to go. For the best canoe trip, put in at a bridge 2 miles upriver on U.S. Route 2. Pull out at the bridge on U.S. Route 8 for a trip to remember. Wildfowl flock to the river at this time of year. A perspective of the gorge from the river is overwhelming. Dozens of places along the river enable you to pull out, picnic, and take it all in—perhaps a deeply therapeutic practice.

Winter brings enjoyable snowshoe and cross-country ski trails. The river carves sculptures out of the rocks and banks, and flowing springs create their own artistry. The surrounding trees

Piers Gorge in the spring is an ideal place for those that like white water sports.

create a very effective windbreak so the area can be taken at leisure. If you're tired of taking the same old trails, you really should do this one. Just remember, the river flows hard under the ice below, so stay well back from the river.

At the junction of U.S. Route 2 and U.S. Route 8 in Norway is a gas station/party store where you can pick up last-minute supplies such as film, munchies, and beverages. Also, a half mile before you hit the Piers Gorge turnoff on U.S. Route 8 resides the small Marion Park. It isn't a place to camp, but it has picnic tables, grills, a water pump, restrooms, and a children's playground. If you're travelling, Marion Park allows you to get your bearings, see the sights, and take a deep breath.

Piers Gorge is one of the treasures of the Iron Mountain area you should check out if in the area. Parking is convenient, so even those on a tight time schedule can enjoy it. You can see a lot of it in an hour or less if you so choose. It's ideal for everyone. Though nestled within an urban and civilized area, this chunk of primordial wilderness will surprise any visitor. More info at http://pointsnorthbooks.com/sites

Porcupine Mountains Ontonagon County

Hikers look across the Lake of the Clouds valley in the Porcupine Mountains

The trails Meander through old-growth forests between the Michigan mountains. Immense moss-covered rock outcrops around every turn dwarf visitors like you. Following alongside are spring-fed streams. As you walk down the mountainsides, small gorges cut by streams grow bigger and wider, the water flowing faster and with increasing volume. Around every bend and turn, sights get more breathtaking, more powerful. Ahead are breaks in the trees, and looming in front—ominous, rugged, and magnificent—is the Escarpment, one of the three formations in the Porcupine Mountains.

The Porcupine Mountains, near Ontonagon, is one of the best-known destinations in Michigan's Upper Peninsula. Many visitors get to view the Lake of the Clouds, one of the only drive-to attractions, and its picture appears in virtually every travel brochure dealing with the state. What most people don't generally see is the heart of the Porcupine Mountains.

The interior of the mountains, diverse and wonderful, is a stronghold for nature in all of its grandeur. Nothing resembles a "Porkie" experience. If you learn what a journey into its heart is like, you can spend much time plotting different unique and wonderful adventures.

Hiking through the Beaver Creek Basin. (top) One of the legendary interior cabins in the Porcupine Mountains. This one is at Mirror Lake. There are several of these throughout the park. (middle) One of Michigan's wildest rivers is the Presque Isle River in the Porcupine Mountains. Magnificent and dangerous it never has a calm moment. (bottom)

the Porkies, once you get there you are essentially on your own. That cannot be overemphasized.

Never leave behind a compass or GPS and waterproof matches. A multi-use fold-up knife, easily carried, could save your life. Know exactly how long the particular trail is, roughly the directions it runs, and its difficulty level. Know if it intersects other trails and where. Maps are essential.

The interior contains dozens of trails. The heart of the Porcupine Mountains is a magical place called Mirror Lake. The interior trails all lead to or from there depending on how you look at it. The major ones are lengthy and require a generous amount of time allotted to the journey. Let's examine them closer.

Union Spring and Union Mine Trails

These trails were created for the visitor with little time who wants to see as much as possible. They are relatively easy and lead to Michigan's second largest freshwater spring. The hiker can walk on a floating bridge to see the water bubbling up from the ground. Also featured is the Union Mine, an 1800s abandoned copper mine, and the Little Union Gorge. With trailheads located off South Boundary Road, these two trails enable visitors to get the feel of what hiking in the Porkies is really like without becoming committed to the depths of the Mountains.

Lost Lake Trail

This trail runs from the South Boundary Road to the Government Peak Trail, following Lost Creek uphill to Lost Lake, a secluded wilderness lake. The walk is beautiful but steep. Once the climb is over, the scenery is breathtaking and worth the hard climb. The trail probably ranks as the most underrated in the park for its dramatic scenery.

Make no mistake. None of this is easy, and no hiker should attempt any of these trails without proper preparations and precautions—mental, physical, and practical. The trails cut through wilderness, and even though frequent visitors trek to the interior of

Summit Peak and South Mirror Lake Trail

Three miles of hard, rough trail run from South Boundary Road to the heart of the mountains. South Mirror Lake Trail begins with a steep climb to the peak of Summit Mountain and has some panoramic views of the Carp River wetlands. The way back down is just as steep. The rest of the way is an average up-and-down hike through hardwoods into the Carp River and Mirror Lake basin. The trail is not easy.

Beaver Creek Trail

The alternative to Summit Peak and South Mirror Lake Trail, Beaver Creek Trail classifies as one of the easiest walking trails the Porkies offer. Hikers will find no scenic overlooks or panoramas that the other trails offer. Instead, the trail goes down into the valleys and wetlands of the Little Carp River. A boardwalk crosses a beaver wetland framed by Summit Peak and smaller mountains. The end of this trail leaves a short and easy walk to either Mirror Lake or Lily Pond.

Lily Pond Trail

The hike on this trail also rates as easy, as no major mountains to get over are on the walk. The route meanders through deep hardwood forests until it comes out at Lily Pond, a picturesque, trout-infested beaver pond. One of the interior cabins is here and well worth a stay.

Little Carp River Trail

Hikers can access the trail through South Boundary Road or the three previous trails. Running from Mirror Lake to Lake Superior, it is one of the longer trails in the park and takes the hiker through virtually every type of terrain the park has. Several waterfalls are along the way, and the Little Carp River provides excel-

The Carp River Basin as seen from the escarpment in the Porcupine Mountains. Our northern rainforest at work.

lent brook trout. Interior cabins at Greenstone Falls in the deep woods provide a gorgeous and serene spot.

Cross Trail

This trail runs between the Little Carp River Trail and the Big Carp River Trail. The hike here is fairly level and uneventful. The highlight of this one is the huge stands of hardwoods and pines. Cabins populate the area where the Cross and Big Carp Trails meet the Lake Superior Trail.

Lake Superior Trail

Lake Superior Trail has the distinction of being the longest trail in the park. Beginning at the far western park boundary at the Presque Isle River and running all the way to M-107 near the Lake of the Clouds, it parallels the shoreline, showcasing Superior as well as the streams that feed it. A lot of low areas and wetlands are along here, so this trail should be avoided during

Lily Pond as seen from the Lily Pond cabin. The heart of the Porcupine Mountains beats here.

peak bug months. This isn't to say that the rest of the Porkies don't have their share, but along this stretch the shore flies have been known to drive early settlers and campers to near madness. Any other time of the year, this trail is breathtaking and worth every step, providing plenty of views and unique scenery that only Lake Superior has. Cabins exist all along the trail as well.

Big Carp River Trail

From one extreme to the next—that's what this trail is. It starts at the Lake of the Clouds scenic-overlook parking lot and runs to Lake Superior. The first section of it follows the edge of the Escarpment and then drops down into the Big Carp River Valley. The hike here is difficult and not recommended for anyone who isn't in good physical shape. If you take it, you will remember the hike for the rest of your life. Many endangered birds nest and hunt along the cliffs of the Escarpment. Frequently, falcons, eagles, vultures, and hawks fly at eye level, circling, hunting, and diving. The

Big Carp River Valley has virgin pine and groves of hardwoods.

Correction Line Trail

Another cut-across trail that runs from the Big Carp River to Mirror Lake, this trail possesses serene wetland and deep woods hikes. It gives the feel of what it is like to hike through isolated wilderness. This trail is deep in the park and meeting other hikers is rare, even in peak season.

North Mirror Lake Trail

This is my favorite trail. It starts at the parking lot at the scenic overlook for the Lake of the Clouds and travels to Mirror Lake. The trail drops steeply into the Big Carp River/Lake of the Clouds basin, providing legendary views. The trail then follows a stream tributary that has created a rock cut that gets more exciting around every bend. Eventually, the trail leads to the source of the stream, which is a flowing spring. A little farther, a stand of thick tall pines welcomes you to Mirror

Sunset clouds over Mirror Lake in the Porkies.

Lake. This trail to me shows nature at her perfection.

Government Peak Trail

This one slices through a section of the mountains few see. It runs from Mirror Lake to the Escarpment and M-107, making for a grueling and magnificent walk. It will take you into the soul of the Porkies through virtually every kind of terrain; the trail meanders along wetlands, the Upper Carp River and the Trap Waterfall, up one of the tallest peaks in Michigan, and into a huge tract of tall, straight, old oaks that have to be seen to be believed.

Escarpment and Overlook Trails

These two, which parallel M-107, don't actually go into the heart of the Porkies, but you sure can see it from the trails. The Escapement Trail begins at the Lake of the Clouds parking lot and follows the edge of the escarpment and comes back out about 4 miles down the road. The Overlook Trail enters at the same place the Escarpment Trail ends and simply makes a long loop back to the same place. The views on these trails are worth the hike. Hikers can see most of the park from above as it spreads out below the sheer cliffs to the horizon. The Overlook Trail is the easier of the pair. The Escarpment Trail offers a hard and at times extremely steep hike, which is recommended for the hiker in sound physical shape.

Cabins and Trailside Accommodations

Hikers can rent designated tent campsites and camping shelters throughout the interior for a nominal fee. They are simple screened-in structures with bunks for two or four. These can be quite a relief if you spend a few days in the interior.

The cabins are fully equipped with bunks and cooking utensils, woodstoves, saws, and axes, and some have boats included also. Vacancies are rare, so plan ahead. They can be reserved up to a year and a half before a trip.

The interior of the Porcupine Mountains is a special place for people looking for a journey into the natural world of Lake Superior wilderness. For more information, see http://www.dnr.state.mi.us/parksandtrails/Details.aspx?id=426&type=SPRK or via http://pointsnorthbooks.com/sites

Portage Bay State Forest Campground Delta County

A quiet and beautiful campground is nestled within great white pines and cedars along the Lake Michigan shoreline on the east side of the Garden Peninsula. Facing east, the bay provides spectacular sunrises as well as privacy. Few visit this gem of the Michigan park system.

Situated just a few miles from Fayette Historical Village, one of Michigan's busiest state parks, Portage Bay can be considered an alternative place for a campsite. It is down 7 miles of dirt road—some of it rough—but through a beautiful forest. Eventually the road becomes the park.

The campground is primitive with pit toilets, but the cost is less than staying at Fayette, and it's less than 10 miles away from Fayette State Park. The campground's 23 sites spread out nicely, so some separation comes between campers. Almost all sites are on the shore, so access to the beautiful sand beach for swimming or paddling, my personal favorite, is right there. The bay is sheltered and faces the sunrise, giving some picturesque Lake Michigan moments.

A public access for boat launching exists, but the launch is sand-surfaced, not cement-padded. Large craft will have real trouble and shouldn't be attempted. Launching anything larger

A storm moves in over Portage Bay.

than a bass boat will result in a tirade of language that most campers won't want to hear.

Though Fayette is a complete ghost town and well worth a visit, a drive around the Garden Peninsula will show that the entire peninsula is dotted with relics. A turn down any side road will go to another lost place that sprung up and thrived during the heyday of the Garden Peninsula. Like many places in the U.P., the ruins and relics stand as monuments to a now gone prosperous past that ended as quickly as it started.

The Garden Peninsula got its name from Native Americans gardening there. Its fisheries and forests provided wood and food for the Chicago region as well

Evening light on the pine plains that surrounds Portage Bay. (top)
Part of the hiking trail at Portage Bay (bottom left)
Osprey on the shore of Portage Bay. Lots of wildlife can be seen here. (bottom right)

as charcoal for smelting pig iron in kilns. Kilns lined the shore of the Garden Peninsula at various points: Sac Bay, Fairport, and Garden Bay. The ore from the iron range was turned into pig iron ingots, which was easier for shipping. The bays were once full with ships loading their cargo as fast as the iron could be smelted. Because the process needed hardwood coals, the Garden Peninsula was stripped of most of its hardwood trees.

The Portage Bay region escaped much of the devastation, being remote and difficult to reach. The forests near the campground still consist of much old growth, which gives the campground a lush and vibrant feel. At the north end of the park is the Ninga Aki Pathway, a combination of two hiking trails: the Lake Michigan Trail, which extends for about a mile and a half, and the Bog Trail, which spans three quarters of a mile. Keep in mind that this is called a bog walk, so take bug repellent. But the pathway will take you through an incredible, almost magical, forest, similar to that of the Lake Michigan Trail, except it has the added bonus of some very nice shoreline views.

Portage Bay offers much solitude and natural beauty. As an alternative to one of the busiest campgrounds in Michigan—Fayette—it can't be beat. It is close enough to be part of a day trip to Big Springs Kitch-iti-kipi in Manistique.

For more information check here: https://www.michigan.org/property/portage-bay-state-forest-campground or via http://pointsnorthbooks.com/sites

Sault Ste. Marie Campgrounds Chippewa County

Many Upper Peninsula parks and recreation areas reside in the quiet, rustic wilderness regions, but others are located right in the midst of hustle and bustle. In Sault Ste. Marie, you can get away from it all, in the midst of it all.

All Sault Ste. Marie campgrounds are located on the shores of the St. Mary's River, a front row for ship viewing. Aune-Osborn Park and the Soo Locks Campground afford incredible views of the ships entering and leaving Soo Locks. Sherman Park, though inside the city, gives the slightly more rustic feel of the upper St. Mary's. Nowhere can these ships be viewed better from the comfort of your lawn chair than at these three places.

Aune-Osborne Park

Located on East Portage Avenue, this campground features one hundred modern (water and electric) campsites. Ships of all kinds sail within a few hundred yards, coming closer as they enter the narrow passage of Sugar Island. Nearby is the Soo's bushplane landing site. Bushplanes frequently visit the St. Mary's waterfront and are a delight to watch. Across the river in Ontario is the Canadian Bushplane Heritage Centre, worth a day excursion.

Freighter leaving the Soo Locks in Sault Ste Marie. (top)
Freighter, Herbert C. Jackson, in a fogbank at Aune Osborne campground. (bottom)

St. Mary's River is well known for its fishing and water sports. Aune-Osborne Park has a boat launch, giving you access to the wonders of the St. Mary's waterway. Fishing is so good on the river that the Masters Walleye Circuit holds an annual event at this park. Yes, in the Soo, even the fishermen go downtown. When fishing and boating

2019 | Points North

in the river, always remember that an international border runs down the middle of it. Crossing it while fishing can be problematic.

Everything here is modern and is set up to handle RVs. Common areas are along the shore, phones are accessible, and you are only a few hundred yards away from one of the legendary eateries in Sault Ste. Marie—Clyde's Drive-In.

Fees at the park are reasonable, though calling in case of changes never hurts. Call 906-632-3268, or visit https://www.saultcity.com/aune-osborn-campground.

Soo Locks Campground

Also located on East Portage Avenue, a mere 12 blocks from the Soo Locks, the Soo Locks Campground where shipmates give you long looks as the ships slow and approach the locks. Nearby is MCM Marine, home of the supply tug *Ojibway,* which resupplies the big freighters. It is a marvel and fascinating to watch. This campground is definitely up close and personal with the ships.

Open from May through October, this campground has one hundred sites too. The sites are modern and include all of the amenities. Common areas on the waterfront allow everyone to enjoy the sights of the St. Mary's and the Locks. Keep in mind that the Soo Locks Campground is pet friendly, a big plus for someone like me who has two Labradors.

The campground accommodates all types of camping structures, from RVs to tents. There are showers and laundry facilities. A game room, gift shop, general store, and lounge area—of course equipped with coffee—give campers things to do even on rainy days. Heck, the campsite even has wireless capability, so you can post all your pictures on Facebook. Don't forget to tag me; I'd like to see them too.

Boat docks available free to all campers, an encouragement to fishermen. This place is a seriously great time waiting to happen.

For information and reservations, call 906-632-3191, or check out its website: http://www.soolockscampground.com/.

Sherman Park

Located off of West Easterday Avenue, Sherman Park is a 68.7-acre park located on the upper St. Mary's River. Though within the city limits, the park is laid out in a rustic, beautiful area along the upper river shore. This is a place for the family to make memories.

A nice beach has handicap access, along with lots of playground equipment. The playground does accommodate adults, with horseshoe pits, basketball hoops, volleyball nets, and even bocce courts. You have to work to be bored here.

The campground has facilities for all types of camping structures, from tents to RVs. Sites come with fire pits. Best of all, the park provides views of ships sailing on the river while you sit under towering pines and maples in your favorite power lounger.

As an added bonus, Sherman Park has nature trails for those that like an occasional hike. Great photo ops appear along here, so don't forget cameras. These hiking trails double as cross-country skiing trails in the winter.

Residents pay lower rates for camping, though nonresidents need only a few dollars more.

You can easily forget you are within the city limits of Sault Ste. Marie. The locale means Sherman Park is minutes from all of the great places to see in the Soo area.

For more information you can call 906-632-5768 or visit its website at https://www.saultcity.com/sherman-park or via http://pointsnorthbooks.com/sites

Seney National Wildlife Refuge and Museum Schoolcraft County

Riding through the man-made wetlands of the Seney Wildlife Refuge is worth the drive every time.

The "Seney Stretch" terrifies the faint of heart. All those familiar with it dread driving that stretch: 25 miles of flat, jack pine wetlands between Seney and Shingleton in Michigan's Upper Peninsula. The drive is considered so boring that stopping for strong coffee before daring to make the crossing is mandatory. But looks can be deceiving.

Behind the scenery at Seney are some amazing things for those who look hard enough. The amount of wildlife concentrated in this area is staggering. Behind those jack pines, and sometimes right in front, is the home for nearly every species of wildlife in Michigan, including rare and endangered species. A visit to the refuge and its museum/headquarters can be very enlightening.

The well-marked entrance to the headquarters, located 3 miles south of M-28 at Seney on M-77, is situated just west of the highway. The US Forest Service has set up a visitor's center that provides details on the Seney area.

The center doubles as a museum. Exhibits depict history, ecology, and wildlife management. Displays include actual specimens of wildlife in the refuge and information on methods of identification, habitats, and habits, along with general information on wildlife and conservation. Dioramas, models, visitor participation boards, movies, photos, and rangers, who are willing to talk, provide various conduits to learning. The tour becomes a comprehensive course on wildlife and why management coupled with environmental protection and conservation is vital, in an admirable mix of education and entertainment.

The Seney National Wildlife Refuge was created in 1935 as a project for the Civilian Conservation Corps (C.C.C.s). When the area was logged in the late 1800s, a wetland and the logged area was left behind. A land syndicate called the Western Land Surety Company bought it and tried to drain the water to create farmland. It didn't work. The surrounding area is a spring-laden swamp that couldn't be drained.

In 1935, Canada Geese were an endangered species, which is hard to believe today, considering that they again fly the sky in abundance. Hunting pressure had nearly decimated the geese, so some kind of nesting area was needed to keep the numbers of geese from failing even more. Hence the Federal Government bought it and assigned the Civilian Conservation Corps to make something out of it. The C.C.C.s built an interlinking system of ponds and streams. When completed, more than seven thousand acres of open water were within 26 ponds or small lakes. The place became dedicated to the preservation, protection, and production of migratory birds and wildlife. The visitor center includes a nice historical display that illustrates the scope of this mammoth project.

A souvenir room holds T-shirts, sweatshirts, and photo prints of wildlife in all sizes, ranging from postcard

A Cedar Waxwing, part of a flock that made the Seney Wildlife Refuge their nesting ground. (top) An Osprey patiently hunts the ponds of the Seney Wildlife Refuge. (bottom)

to poster. Stationery and trinkets are offered for sale. All money, after covering costs, helps maintain the center and refuge.

The rangers provide good insight into their goals and basic purposes. Docu-

A Trumpeter Swan family on the edge of one of the wildlife ponds at the Seney Wildlife Refuge.

mentation and data collected on both endangered and common species fills volumes, much of it provided by visitors. A log is kept with different species sightings by visitors to the refuge. The rangers state 80 percent of all information on Michigan wildlife comes from the Seney Refuge and proves invaluable. Visitors can find Information on virtually every species of wildlife, native or passing through.

The refuge is open to visitors. A 7-mile drive, built by the Forest Service, cuts through bayous and wetlands that make up most of the Seney landscape. The abundance of wildlife seen is unexpected and staggering: nesting bald eagles, trumpeter swans, beaver, song birds, turtles, wolves, and deer, to name a few. All can be seen in a drive around the refuge. Turnouts along the road allow walking and observing refuge wildlife at a leisurely pace and at close range. A camera is a must for this visit.

For the more ambitious visitor, the Forest Service provides hiking trails, offering even more rare views of wild-life. Limited hunting and fishing are allowed on the refuge. Very stringent rules must be followed to the letter. More information can be obtained by writing Seney National Wildlife Refuge, HCR2, Box 1, Seney, Michigan 49883.

Canoeing is allowed on the outer reaches of the refuge and is a productive means to view wildlife. Rentals are available in Germfask, 13 miles south of the visitors' center. The Manistique River cuts through this town and the heart of the refuge. Several navigable tributaries provide additional miles of exploring and pleasure.

For winter buffs, cross-country skiing, snowshoeing, and ice fishing are allowed, but snowmobiles are not. No trails are groomed; still, the area provides something different for a winter day or weekend. Investigate the refuge for even more possibilities.

Wildlife abounds in the Seney Stretch. Instead of lamenting the bleak drive, watch closely for a glimpse of its beauty and wildlife. Check the website at http://www.fws.gov/refuge/seney or via http://pointsnorthbooks.com/sites

Seul Choix Pointe Lighthouse Park and Museum Schoolcraft County

The first thing that stands out about Seul Choix Lighthouse is how well the restoration was done. After so many lighthouses have fallen into ruin, this one stands majestically, its red-brick and white tower gleaming against the blue sky of summer.

The shoreline of the Great Lakes boasts many lighthouses that have played a vital role in safe shipping and are focal points of history unique to the Great Lakes and its small communities. Seul Choix is no exception.

Seul Choix means "only choice" in French; voyageurs (boatmen working for fur companies) dubbed the area that. It is pronounced sel-shwa.

Seul Choix's past, which includes Native Americans, voyageurs, commercial fishermen, and lightkeepers, is long and difficult. The Gulliver Historical Society, founded in 1987, has retraced and recorded the area's past and has used the lighthouse as a means for historical preservation. The lighthouse and surrounding buildings are a museum and storehouse for artifacts, pictures, and historical information.

Lighthouse with bird house replica

View from tower (top)
Lighthouse interior (bottom left)
Lighthouse interior (bottom right)

The town of Gulliver is located on U.S. Route 2, 11 miles east of Manistique. The lighthouse is 8 miles south of Gulliver. Its turnoff is off U.S. Route 2 and is well marked by signs reading "Historic Lighthouse." Like many of the locations along the Great Lakes, it is pleasant and quiet.

The Seul Choix Point Lighthouse complex is one of the most picturesque lighthouses on the Great Lakes as well as one of the few still complete. Not only is the light tower still intact, but also the entire main house where two families once lived has been restored to its original condition, and several outbuildings containing vivid displays have been fully restored.

In 1988, the society began restoration inside the building that used to house the old foghorn. After tearing out remnants of machinery in January with no heat, workers pulled down layers of hammered tin that covered the ceiling, and an accumulation of 93 years of bat dung came down too. Needless to say, it wasn't a pleasant or healthy experience. The dedicated workers then refinished the interior to create a historical museum. The building wasn't large, but they made a start.

Members of the community donated many artifacts that had been squirreled away in attics, and some of the original settlers' relatives, who no longer lived in the area, sent items. Displays took shape, and soon the small outbuilding was filled and a visual history assembled. Many of the artifacts are classic and in excellent condition. A number of photographs were unearthed, identified, and arranged, providing a visual image of the past. From these humble beginnings, Seul Choix Lighthouse was slowly but steadily brought back to life.

The displays reflect the difficult life along the Lake Michigan shore. Throughout the lighthouse, the rooms burst with reflections of lighthouse life. Climbing the 99 steps to the top of the tower is a bit of an effort, but the view of Lake Michigan, Seul Choix Pointe itself, and the freighters coming in for the limestone mine across the bay more than make up for it.

Seul Choix Lighthouse and Museum.

Some artifacts and relics unearthed at Seul Choix have been major discoveries. One artifact, a dugout canoe made of a solid piece of wood, is one of the rarest artifacts to be uncovered in the Midwest. The canoe is believed to be of French origin and is the only one of its kind discovered in the Midwest. *National Geographic* magazine, upon learning of the canoe, sent a photographer to Gulliver, lending further credence to the importance of the discovery. It has been dated to colonial era.

Some of the society's "discoveries" include remains of Ottawa and Chippewa Indian fishing villages along the beach—old foundations and skeletons of huts. Paintings on rocks and in caves have been found. Reconstructing one of the native fishing villages onsite at the lighthouse is being considered.

The society found an inscribed rock carving left by French trapper Louis Metty. Another rock carving on the lakeshore is believed to have been left by a lighthouse keeper's son.

Another of the society's important discoveries is what is believed to be a sunken schooner, buried just off-

shore in the sand. The bow is exposed in about five feet of water. By poking a long rod in the sand, workers determined the schooner is about 120 feet long. A query to the Great Lakes Maritime Historical Society resulted in a list of possible identities for the wreck though none have been positively determine.

All quality lighthouses have a ghost, and Seul Choix has a quality ghost—an old lightkeeper who appears in uniform. He has even protected the lighthouse by running off thieves. Because of all the ghost sightings, the lighthouse has hosted paranormal investigations, and one of the founders of the Gulliver Historical Society, Marilyn Fischer has two books on hauntings called "Spirits of Seul Choix Pointe, True Lighthouse Stories Vols. 1 and 2.

Seul Choix is also the scene of a landmark murder case. In 1859, Augustus Pond, a local fisherman who had moved to Seul Choix from Mackinac Island, was being harassed by some of the locals. It got so bad that Pond actually feared for his life. One night, his fish

Rare French dugout canoe is on display at Seul Choix.

shanty was raided and destroyed, and his house was attacked. He came out of his house with a shotgun loaded with pigeon shot and fired after the raiders. One of them dropped dead. On inspection, Pond discovered he'd killed the son of the local judge! He knew a fair trial was out of the question. When the case went to trial at Mackinac Island, Pond was naturally convicted and sentenced to 10 years in prison. His lawyer didn't give up and took Pond's case to the Supreme Court. In a landmark decision, the court ruled that a man had a right to defend himself and his home if he felt threatened, even with deadly force. The decision is still used in defense trials to this day. Pond's conviction was overturned, and he was set free.

In the gift shop, an audiovisual room shows a documentary on the history on display throughout the lighthouse and orients the visitor to the historical context. This should be viewed and helps put a timeline for all of the displays.

A picnic area on the grounds of the lighthouse provides a quiet setting on the shore of Lake Michigan overlooking a beautiful bay. No overnight camping is allowed, but campgrounds are in nearby Manistique.

The Gulliver Historical Society plans improvements for years to come. A possibility is to move some of the original homesteads onto the property and refurbish and return them to their original state. They would house displays and artifacts reflecting the lifestyles of the original settlers.

Seul Choix Pointe helped define the Upper Peninsula and our country. A trip to the Lighthouse Museum should be a priority on the travel list. The Gulliver Historical Society has created a window to the past that leaves the viewer enriched and fascinated with the unique history of Seul Choix. For more information on the Seul Choix Lighthouse Museum or the Gulliver Historical Society, call 906-283-3317, or email msfischer@hughes.net or visit http://pointsnorthbooks.com/sites

Museum of Ojibwa Culture
Mackinac County

The Museum of Ojibwa Culture in St. Ignace.

The Museum of Ojibwa Culture, in Sainte Ignace toward the east end of town at the north end of the boardwalk, displays and explains an aspect of Great Lakes life that predates all else, that of the Native American. It is located at the gravesite of Father Marquette, now called the Father Marquette Mission Park, where he established his mission for a village of displaced Hurons, the natives he discovered living there.

The Mackinaw Straits area of Michigan is one of the most historically significant in the United States and draws nearly a million visitors a year. History still remains, and is continuously reenacted, at both Mackinaw City in Fort Michilimackinac and on Mackinac Island at Fort Mackinac. The history of Europeans in America began here in the late 1600s with the coming of Jesuit explorer Jacques Marquette, making it one of the first places to be settled in

Also located at the Museum of Ojibwa Culture is the grave of the legendary Jesuit explorer and priest, Father Marquette. (top) The Museum of Ojibwa Culture shows how Natives lived before European influence changed their lives. (bottom)

the United States. St. Ignace holds the key to the oldest of that history.

The history shows the impact of early settlements and the military affairs between the British and the French for control of the Great Lakes, but Native Americans were in the area for about ten thousand years. Long before any European ever dreamed of a new world, a civilization and way of life were in place.

Native Americans knew every aspect of the natural surroundings and lived in harmony with it. The Ojibwa, the natives of this region, allowed the Europeans to coexist with them when they finally arrived.

If a visitor to the area really wants to understand the region's history, not just the European aspects when the British and the French came, he or she needs to experience the Museum of Ojibwa Culture. The displays include archaeological finds, videos, and models.

This location has been considered not only one of the most important archaeological sites in the Midwest but also the oldest. The digs have uncovered thousands of artifacts, the outlines of several longhouses, and the remains of fire hearths, storage pits, and refuse areas.

Upon entering the museum, formerly St. Ignace's oldest church, you are greeted with eight-foot photo enlargements of natives and a large partition display that explains the original legend of the Ojibwa migration, which led the tribe to the area. Those tribal members are the original people of the upper Great Lakes region, whose ancestors were scattered through Ontario, Michigan, Wisconsin, and Minnesota.

Throughout the museum, the visitor finds displays of many of the artifacts dug up on the site. Interpretive signs explain what they are, their use, and the spiritual meanings behind them. Native Americans were highly spiritual people; their daily lives and tools all had meaning and purpose. They had adapted amazingly to the harshness of the Great Lakes environment.

A reproduced hut sits inside the museum, with a short video explaining the ways and family structure of the Ojibwa. The highly detailed display and video tie everything together. It has interviews with area natives and not only speaks of life historically but also comments on where Native Americans are now.

Toward the end of the displays, more artifacts and interpretation document the impact of the missionaries. Discus-

Interior displays present an overview of different aspects of Native life.

sion here concerns how the imposition of Christianity irreversibly changed their culture.

This museum is wonderfully done and surprisingly complete for its small size. Outside in the courtyard, a longhouse (a type of traditional Native American dwelling) stands onsite, and an interpretive garden walk familiarizes the visitor with Native uses for herbs and plants. Development plans include partial reconstruction of the Huron village.

More extensive exhibits are planned on the Huron and Odawa Natives, regarding how they adapted to displacement from their homeland by the Iroquois in the 1640s. They had established several villages in the upper Great Lakes area.

The museum cost is small—a couple dollars as the high price. Elementary students, tour groups, and families qualify for discounts. The museum is open from Memorial Day to late October.

A Native American gift shop features traditional Ojibwa arts, crafts, and literature. Authentic artisans make the arts and crafts, and the work is magnificent as well as educational. Many of the drawings and books are inspired by native legends and tales.

When visiting or travelling through the Straits of Mackinac and St. Ignace, make sure to take some time to visit the Marquette Mission Park and Museum of Ojibwa Culture. Your understanding of the significance of the Straits area and the Upper Peninsula as a whole will never be complete without it. See http://museumofojibwaculture.net or via http://pointsnorthbooks.com/sites

Stonington Peninsula Delta County

The limestone cliffs at the Stonington Peninsula.

Thinking about a vacation or taking off for a weekend? Tired of the same old places? The Stonington Peninsula, situated south of Rapid River, could be the place for you. Much of the area is a part of the Little Bay de Noc Recreation Area, one of the finest areas for every kind of outdoor activity, especially during warm weather. Stonington contains thousands of acres of United States forestland, only a small portion of the Hiawatha National Forest. The National Forest Service maintains areas here for activities.

The area dates back to the early 1800s, and prior to then supported a large Native American population. With diverse beauty, habitat, and recreation possibilities, the region offers camping, picnic areas, beaches, fishing, hiking, and scenic drives and, of course, it has a lighthouse. The traveler's limitations are due only to the imagination.

The doorway to the peninsula is Delta County Road 513, located 3 miles east of Rapid River, branching from U.S. Route 2. The county road runs about 18 miles and dead-ends at a point protruding into Lake Michigan, where a lighthouse sits. The abundant national forestland bordering this road welcomes public use.

The regional office of the United States Forest Service is conveniently located between Rapid River and County Road 513 on U.S. Route 2. Visitors to the area should stop there for precise location of all U.S.F.S. property. Area rules and maps are available. The staff is friendly and helpful, always willing to steer visitors to areas and accesses that assure maximum benefit from the visit regardless of favorite activities.

The U.S.F.S. has set up and regularly maintains three specific areas. The first, Little Bay de Noc Campground, is located about 7 miles up County Road 513. The turnoff to the right is marked clearly and is just past the sign for Hunter's Point Boat Launch, a public access to Lake Michigan.

Once inside the Bay de Noc Campground, you will see the reward for the effort immediately. The campground, located on Lake Michigan, has a lovely sand beach, and most of the sites have shore access. Picnic tables, outhouses, and water pumps are in place, with ample places to set up camp.

There is the Maywood History Trail hike that winds through the park past old foundations and through the dense trees. Interpretive signs show where Native Americans camped. The remains of the old Maywood Resort are a highlight of this short trail.

The second must-see location is the Squaw Creek Old Growth Area, 3 miles beyond the park turnoff. The spot is well marked, and 513 runs over and across Squaw Creek. Here, Squaw Creek runs through one of the oldest stands of trees remaining in Delta County, affording infinite photographic opportunities around every corner. A well-known trout stream for fishermen, the creek is especially enjoyable to the hiker. The miles and miles of trail that run through a diversity of landscapes and habitats make a memorable experience only found in the Old Growth. When visiting, remember that this is

Remains of an old seabed can be found at Stonington Point along the shore. (top) The lighthouse at Stonington Point open to the public. (bottom)

a research area, so exercise care. The ecology is rare and fragile.

From here the road travels along the lakeshore, skirting Little Bay de Noc, toward the once-thriving town of Stonington. A couple of buildings mark the ghost town, which is mostly a flat treeless field. A little further down the road, more relic buildings appear, showing evidence of another small ghost town.

The shoreline is made up of sheer, tall cliffs—layered, hard-packed clay

Remnants of old ghost towns can be seen along the Stonington Peninsula. (top)
An old store front still stands where an old ghost town used to be on the Stonington Peninsula. (bottom)

pressed into stone. Unique to the area, the cliffs decorate much of the peninsula's shoreline. At the foot of the cliffs, a narrow shoreline permits walking, and views from the bottom are majestic. Where the road runs close to the edge, one may pull over, get out, and take a rewarding look.

Following the road to the end affords another spot for fun—the Peninsula Point Lighthouse (a USFS historical site). A lighthouse and keeper's residence formerly stood here. Built in 1872, it eventually burned. Nothing is left except the light tower itself, a real attraction because it is open. A climb up the wrought iron stair to the top where the light was housed provides a feeling of what it was like when operational. At the top, the view of Lake Michigan, Little Bay de Noc, and surrounding woods is breathtaking. On the tower grounds are picnic tables, a groomed lawn, water and outhouse facilities. There is no camping. The Stonington Peninsula Point Lighthouse area is also a monarch butterfly hatching ground. When they hatch, they hang like clusters of orange and black fruit as they dry their wings. Hundreds of thousands hatch there every year.

The shore west of the tower contains a clay layer that makes up the cliffs at Stonington. Its attraction is countless imbedded brachiopods, fossilized prehistoric shelled organisms similar to a clam. Mixed in are remains of prehistoric grasses and reeds, well preserved and recognizable.

The last mile of road leading to lighthouse point is not recommended for vehicles over 8 feet high and 16 feet long. Cars can easily travel the dirt, two-rut road, making quite a scenic drive. Several turnouts for cars, trucks, and trailers to set up camp fall along the stretch. The lakeshore here is a long sand beach, ideal for swimming.

Opportunities for enjoyment are unlimited; the preceding are just highlights. Days can be spent without repeating activities. Two stores along County Road 513 offer supplies; major supply stocking should be done at Rapid River.

Besides being a warm-weather area, the peninsula presents opportunity for cross-country skiing, snowshoeing, and snowmobiling. The USFS has created specialized wildlife habitats, so hunting is excellent. Ruffed grouse, hare, and deer populations are high.

After your initial visit, be careful—travel here can become a habit. More info at http://pointsnorthbooks.com/sites

Sturgeon River Gorge Wilderness Baraga County

The Sturgeon River Waterfall is in the heart of the gorge a scene not to be missed.

A millennium of natural creation has left one of the most spectacular sights of the Upper Peninsula. Dubbed the "Grand Canyon" of the U.P., the Sturgeon River Gorge Wilderness is mile after mile of the best of remote wilderness. Fortunately, getting there isn't difficult, and the scenery and views are breathtaking, making this region a popular destination for the locals who know about it. It can be enjoyable any time of the year, but fall will send a visitor away with the knowledge of having viewed a true wonder.

The Sturgeon River Gorge Wilderness is carved out of approximately 20 miles of land between M-38 and M-28, 12 miles southwest of Baraga. This section is remote, and few signs let you know that you're on the right trail. You will have to be something of an explorer to enjoy

One of the U.P.'s great scenic rivers, the Sturgeon River runs through the heart of the peninsula.

it, but the effort will be well worth it. It is isolated and magnificent. The roads are all good throughout. They are dirt, but they are graded and passable with any vehicle.

To get there, go west of Baraga on M-38 for about 10 miles, and turn right after the road crosses the Sturgeon River. Travel south for 8 miles, past the Prickett Dam and backwater; this is the Sturgeon dammed up. Another couple miles will get you into the Silver Mountain vicinity—the first sight in the wilderness area, which should be seen.

Another route into the area is near Sidnaw on M-28. One-half mile east of Sidnaw, a dirt road goes to the north, right after the airport. Drive a little over 2 miles to a fork in the road. Take the right-hand road; after about 3.5 miles, a small campground will be on the left-hand side—the beginning of the gorge on the south end. This area once held a World War II German prison camp, and once you make it out here you will easily see why.

Between Silver Mountain and the campground you will find spectacular scenery rarely seen by the traditional U.P. visitor. A variety of Michigan mountains and high rock bluffs populate the range. Several scenic pullouts are here but are unmarked. You'll have to do some of your own exploring. Some of the many trails that lead toward the river will come out at overlooks, while others will wind down into the lower elevations.

Once you establish basic familiarity with the gorge, knowing the region more intimately won't take long. The road follows the general course of the river, so any trails heading its direction will access a different section of the Sturgeon.

Though recreational activities along the Sturgeon River are limited, the area is one of the finest to enjoy the possible ones. Each season has its own charm and unique character. Hiking, fishing, white-water rafting, snowmobiling, off-road vehicle touring, snowshoeing, cross-country skiing, large-game hunting, and sightseeing are all enjoyed in the area.

The North Country Trail runs along this section of river, giving unrestricted foot access to the valleys and cliffs. Virtually every part of the river is accessible. For backpackers and hikers, this trail offers everything. It is strenuous enough to test skills, no matter the level of hiker. Moderate sections and hard scrambling steep inclines exist. Road accesses are close enough that hikers can chose from a variety of distances and difficulties so that most can find some portion, if not several, that will please them.

The trail is a boon for fishermen too. The Sturgeon River is an excellent trout stream through this area. Rocky and wide, it provides fly and bait anglers a memorable fishing excursion. Sections of waterfalls, white water, and holes have over the years produced many large catches. Spring, summer, and fall are prime fishing months.

Winter of course provides incomparable snowshoeing and cross-country skiing. The gorge is ungroomed, so the experience is isolated and exhaustive—perhaps exactly the challenge you are looking for. Once back in the gorge, the scenery is breathtaking, with all of the majesty that ice and snow can deliver. Tall cliffs decorate with massive icicles from flowing and freezing springs.

Riverside campsite (top)
Bear Den overlook (bottom)

Deep, massive drifts of snow adorn the ledges and summits. The constantly flowing river continuously creates sculptures of the natural forms along the riverbed. Access this time of year is by snowmobile only. The roads are seasonal but worth the effort.

Springtime's rushing white water tempts paddlers, but sections of the river are closed because they are too dangerous. Research is a must. One sign warns that "while the river below here is of intermediate skill level, difficult water occurs about 1.5 miles before the Sturgeon River Falls. A more difficult ledge drop occurs just before the falls itself. It is imperative to be on the river right and take out above this faster wa-

The dilapidated stairway to the top of Silver Mountain, soon to be removed.

ter or risk being swept over the falls to a probable death. Water below the falls is continuously more difficult. Scout all rapids before running them!" Fast and treacherous, the Sturgeon River is for those who really want to challenge a river. The frequent road access makes it convenient for support vehicles.

This brings me to one of the most spectacular sites in the Sturgeon River Gorge Wilderness, the Sturgeon River Falls. This breathtaking section of river can be accessed from the Forest Road. The hike is about a mile and is a switchback downhill, uphill on the way out. Once there, spending time taking in the river, the falls, and the surrounding scenery of high bluffs will grip your soul. It has become a personal favorite that I return to time and time again.

Because of the extensive system of forest service roads, the area is ideal for off-road vehicles (though beware of some roads closed to ATVs) and snowmobiles. The Sturgeon River Gorge Wilderness is fast becoming an attraction among trail riders. Off-roaders are allowed as long as they stay on the designated trails. The routes are nicely laid out, highlighting the gorge extensively.

For sightseers, the pullouts provide views of the expansive valleys the river has carved. For this, fall has the most impact. A climb to the top of Silver Mountain will allow you to see all the way back to Baraga and then some. The effort is worth it, but the stairway up is in need of repair, and caution must be taken. The Forest Service has commented they may just remove it since Silver Mountain attracts a lot of rock climbers. Pins can be seen in the rocks on the way up. If the stairs is gone, a bit of creative maneuvering on the rocks can still get one to the summit. The summit is basically bare, so looks can be taken from any direction. With the fall colors, there's nothing like it. The forest canopy is of thick hardwood and pine mix, which adds diversity of color that goes completely unnoticed in color-tour recommendations.

The campground on the south end of the gorge is a beautiful little rarely used site. Positioned on a bend in the Sturgeon, it's a pleasant place to spend some time. Only a few sites are here, but camping costs nothing. Picnic tables, fire pits, vault toilets, and hand-pumped freshwater are provided. The sites are primitive with no hookups, but if you like roughing it a bit, this can be a place for you.

If you like to do some exploring and investigating, what can be discovered here is rewarding. Experience the U.P.'s Grand Canyon. More info at http://pointsnorthbooks.com/sites

Twin Lakes State Park Houghton County

It started as the getaway for two Houghton businessmen, Roland and Gerald Wright, the sons of a Keweenaw magnate, Charles Wright, who owned the Copper Range Railroad and the Superior National Bank in Houghton. The pair recognized a different kind of wealth in the region—that of relaxation. The two lakes suited the pair, and the lakes were named after each of them: Lake Roland and Lake Gerald. (The names remain to this day.) Eventually, a small village and resort community sprang up. The railroad ran past, so it was easy to travel in from Houghton. Some of the old buildings from this early era can be seen at Twin Lakes still. A state park now sits on the shore of Lake Gerald, and as those two brothers did, all can enjoy the area

Quiet, out of the way, picturesque—all describe Twin Lakes State Park. Like many places in the Upper Peninsula, the park offers plenty during any season: hiking, sightseeing, fishing, boating, and, during warmer months, swimming.

Twin Lakes reminds me of those places my parents liked to take me to, where I can thrive through fun and curiosity. Situated between Houghton and Ontonagon, the park is designed

The hidden Wyandotte Falls near Twin Lakes.

House from Winona. (top)
Mine tailings pile from one of the old mines
from the ghost town of Winona near Twin Lakes.
(bottom)

One of the well-kept secrets of this area, the park is fully equipped. An extensive playground entertains the kids with swings, slides, teeter-totters, merry-go-rounds, and a supervised beach. A small nature/hiking trail is well worth the minimal effort.

The park contains 160 campsites, which accommodate everything from RVs to tents. Fully modern facilities include showers and changing rooms.

A cabin available for rent comes with most camping necessities, such as dishes, an axe, a handsaw, and a mattress. Prospective renters must call ahead to make reservations. The price ranks as one of the most inexpensive. The park also has a lodge building, perfect for meetings and large family get-togethers.

The lakes, famed for their fishing, teem with pan fish, bass, and pike. A public access within the park will accommodate small to medium boats. The lake here has many shallow spots, so larger cabin-style boats would be unsuitable. Paddling here is incredible, and going from one lake to another is a nice day paddle.

For a side trip, consider a drive to Misery Bay or Agate Beach, both on Lake Superior about a half hour away. Both places have their own picnic areas and sandy beaches. These two remote spots are scenic in the extreme; even if you're driving through, they're worth a detour.

Even many locals are unaware of a particular beautiful waterfall. Turn off M-28 onto Lake Road toward the golf course. Go past the course, and on the left a small sign reads, "Wyandotte Falls." Park and follow the short trail; you will be rewarded.

Ghost towns are close at hand as well. Donken, a former lumbering town, lies 5 miles to the east of Twin Lakes. Win-

for getaway and play and is also relaxing. It is 5 miles west of Toivola on M-28. You can't miss it.

The playground at Twin Lakes State Park. (top)
Lake Roland as seen from Krupp's Resort. (bottom)

ona, formerly a copper-mining village, lies about 5 miles to the west.

Twin Lakes is open all year and is worth visiting anytime. Fall makes the area a candidate for a fine color tour. Late-year fishing is excellent, and the area abounds with all types of game animals for hunting.

Sandwiched between the Porcupine Mountains and Copper Country—both only a 30-mile drive away—and offering plenty to do, Twin Lakes State Park amounts to a fine choice. What more could anyone want? More info at http://pointsnorthbooks.com/sites

Tyoga Historical Pathway
Alger County

T he history of Michigan's Upper Peninsula is filled with tales of rags to riches to rags again. Towns rose and fell; people came and left. More often than not, the glory lasted merely a few years. Evidence of these places and tales are scattered in every corner and county. The Tyoga Historical Pathway, a hiking trail through the location of a ghost town, shows off one of those ghost towns.

Located in Alger County between Marquette and Munising on the banks of the scenic Laughing Whitefish River, the pathway is 2 miles north of M28 at Deerton. The turnoff is 200 feet east of the Laughing Whitefish River off M-28. A small wooden sign marks the turn. The road is gravel but it's good quality and any vehicle shouldn't have trouble. The entrance will be on the right side about 2 miles.

A 1.4-mile interpretive hiking trail reveals the entire history of a frontier town through a guided tour of the various sites where the town stood. No buildings remain, but through photographs and historical descriptions along the trail, the old town comes to light.

Tyoga didn't last very long. Founded around 1900, its entire history spans a little over a decade before it was abandoned. Like many other UP communi-

Bridge over the Laughing Whitefish River on the Tyoga Historical Pathway. (top)
The graves of lumberjacks who lost their lives working in the woods. (bottom)

ties, it flourished while the resources held out but then withered as employment moved on.

Life here centered around logging. Immense mixed growth of pine and hardwoods provided work for two continuous cutting crews and profits for the Tyoga lumber mill. The mill,

Much of the pathway is on old railroad grades. Some of the track left for hikers shows how the old railroad ran through the dense woods.

located along the Laughing Whitefish River, took 40 men to operate. An immense steam engine ran a band saw that could cut 50 thousand board feet a day. The mill paid its workers $1.75 a day for ten hours of work. A worker could find lodgings for 25 cents a day, which included the laundry. In 1906, a game warden from Soo cited the lumber mill for dumping its sawdust and garbage into the stream, violating turn-of-the-century environmental laws.

The lumberjacks were mainly Finns, Englishmen, and French-Canadians, a rough bunch prone to drinking and fighting. The men were divided into two separate crews, and between them they cut down all the timber surrounding Tyoga.

The largest of the crews, run by an Irishman named Dan McEachern, consisted of 32 lumberjacks and four women cooks. The lumberjacks were devoted solely to cutting huge virgin pine trees that were four to five feet in diameter. The 150-foot trees shook the earth all over town when they fell. The lumber mill harvested more than 60 million board feet of lumber from the seven thousand acres the company owned.

At its peak, Tyoga consisted of 150 residents in plank houses and log cabins, along with a company store, boarding house, blacksmith, cook shanty, horse barns, and the sawmill along the river. In 1906 the town received a post office, and in 1908 it built a school.

A railroad spur of the Duluth, South Shore, and Atlantic Railway bisected the town, bringing supplies and carrying visitors in and lumber away. Many residents lived off the abundant venison and 3.5-pound trout from the river.

In 1907 the mill was sold to Cleveland-Cliffs Iron Company along with the acreage. C.C.I. dismantled the mill and the next year moved it to Munising so all of C.C.I.'s operations could have a more central location. Later it burned in Munising.

This was the beginning of the end for Tyoga. In 1908 the mill was gone, and only a few families remained. By 1911, the town was completely abandoned. A sleigh-and-horse team moved the schoolhouse along the railroad grade to Deerton, where it still stands.

The Tyoga Historical Pathway provides a pleasant walk along the Laughing Whitefish River basin and then turns into the woods. Some excellent stands of old growth pines and hardwoods endure here. The walk isn't difficult, and with the interpretive signs, it turns out to be leisurely. A good eye can spot old foundations and a piece of railroad that marks the line that once serviced the old town. The woods contain graves of loggers killed accidentally. Large open meadow spaces remain where the buildings of the old town once stood. Interpretive signs give a good overall view of how the town once appeared. It is easy to envision the life of the village in the days of its height. The Tyoga history parallels so many other early UP communities, the Tyoga location reflects them all. More info at http://pointsnorthbooks.com/sites

Woodland Park
Alger County

Grand Marais harbor a few blocks from Woodland Park. (top)
Grand Sable Falls near Woodland Park in Grand Marais. (bottom left)

The long sand and stone beach stretches to the horizon. Tall sand dunes tower above the shoreline, stoic, watchful. Lake Superior shimmers in the sunlight, creating a mist that will turn into an evening fog. Under the lake lie the remains of countless wrecks from the unforgiving violence of storms. A cool breeze floats across the beach, cooling the setting summer sun. Already the sun accents the dunes with orange, pink, and lavender. Evening falls on Woodland Park.

Grand Sable Dunes

Located in the north side of the harbor village Grand Marais, the park is set above the beach in a stand of mixed pines and hardwoods. This picturesque campground overlooks the breathtaking Lake Superior beach that evolves into the Grand Sable Dunes making up the western horizon. Grand Marais has everything any traveler could hope for: a grocery store, hardware, restaurants, a coffee shop, a party store with gas, and gift shops.

Grand Marais harbor is ideal for any water sports. Fishing boats, Jet Skis, kayaks, and swimmers all skim across the bay. The abundance of wrecks (the area is also known as the shipwreck coast) make Grand Marais a diver's paradise. Grand Marais is also designated as a harbor of refuge, which means it is normally sheltered from heavy seas by land and provides safe navigation and mooring.

The marina at the Grand Marais harbor will accommodate most sizes of pleasure boats. Boaters may use well-maintained launching facilities for a fee. No permanent slips (slopes leading into water) are in the park, gas is available, and many boaters tie to the dock during their stay.

Woodland Park is right in the middle of one of the world's longest and highest beaches and marks the east end of Pictured Rocks National Lakeshore. Pictured Rocks is a backpacker's staple. Consequently, well-marked and developed hiking trails run between some of the area's finest attractions, making them easily accessible. Places like the Hurricane River with Au Sable Point Lighthouse, the Log Slide Overlook, Twelve Mile Beach, Grand Sable Falls, and Grand Sable Lake are just a beachstone's throw from Grand Marais.

Woodland Park is fully equipped with camping facilities, and also a few extras. Fully modern hookups (electricity, water, dump station) for campers and RVs are available, along with shower facilities. A playground exists for kids

The wind can get a bit out of hand here. Grand Marais Pier being battered by Lake Superior.

and the Grand Marais recreation center is next to the park. So a softball field, basketball court, and tennis court are next to the park, and in town, down on the beach, are volleyball nets.

Fishing is excellent all throughout the area, from deep lake trout and salmon fishing on Lake Superior to trout fishing on any of the rivers. The Sucker and Hurricane rivers provide steelhead and salmon runs. The Hurricane's runs are legendary in the area, and, of course, the Fox River, where Ernest Hemingway enjoyed the brook trout he caught, is to the south of Grand Marais. Grand Sable Lake has good catches of northern pike, bass, and other pan fish. The lake has a medium boat-launch ramp, provided by the U.S. Park Service, which will accommodate most boats 17 feet or under.

While fishing or just on an outing, keep your eye open for an eagle nested on the south end of Grand Sable Lake. Catching sight of her can be a breathtaking experience for the entire family.

Grand Marais is north of Seney at the end of M-77. Drive into Grand Marais. Keep going through town, past the Dunes Saloon and the Bayshore Market, and turn left at the next block. A few hundred feet down the street is Woodland Park. The cost is minimal, and the stay is priceless.

Other points of interest in the Grand Marais area are the Lightkeeper's House Museum at Coast Guard Point; the Grand Marais School Forest, which has hiking trails and Sucker River access for fishermen; the Pickle Barrel House Museum, with visitor information center and gift shop; and the Gitchee Gumee Agate and History Museum. You could always hunt for agate and driftwood along the miles of beach. Gather the blueberries and raspberries that grow in abundance, or explore the countless miles of trails through the woods. The North Country Trail also runs through here (a map is mandatory).

Dozens of small hidden lakes, streams, wetlands, and forests fill the area. A lifetime of adventures wait to be discovered or rediscovered here. Once you find it, Woodland Park will become a regular destination on your journeys through the U.P. More info at http://pointsnorthbooks.com/sites

Whitefish Point Maritime Museum Chippewa County

Whitefish Point Lighthouse which now houses the Great Lakes Shipwreck Museum.

Massive waves crash over the sides of the floundering freighter. Men scramble to protect the ship from the pounding of the enraged Lake Superior. The vessel is taking on water three times as fast as the pumps can push it back out. The situation is getting dire. The crew knows that it is only a matter of time until the lake will swallow their vessel and, very possibly, them. The life ropes that had been strung around the ship for support and grip in the storm were now constantly engulfed in blowing water and crashing waves. Wind, rain and pounding surf makes the captain's orders unintelligible, but the men know what is said. It is the abandon ship order. The lifeboats are uncovered but suddenly they are all awash,

The notorious Whitefish Point and the wonderful beach at the Great Lakes Shipwreck Museum. (top)
The walls tell stories here. This one about a treasure ship at the Great Lakes Shipwreck Museum. (bottom)

to Sault Sainte Marie, makes it an area of extreme danger for the crews of freighters and pleasure craft. Adverse weather compounds the chances for tragedy, making the area infamous. It's known as the graveyard of the Great Lakes.

Whitefish Point Lighthouse, a crucial participant in Lake Superior's history, has become a showcase for the history of the lighthouse and the surrounding area, presenting an image of itself and the past that is worthy of its subject matter. The Great Lakes Shipwreck Society has turned it into a maritime museum that is fascinating. On display are various artifacts, photos, models and videos documenting the shipwrecks that have occurred in the area.

Whitefish Point lies 11 miles north of Paradise on Wire Road. It's the only good road going north - a winding, asphalt road that skirts the shoreline, providing scenic views of Lake Superior and sand beaches. As you drive along, you can't help but wonder how such a picturesque section of the lake can be the scene of so much tragedy.

After passing an old building that used to be the area's oldest post office, one rounds a curve, and peeking out between the pines is the Whitefish Point Lighthouse.

The Great Lakes Shipwreck Society has created one of the finest museums in Michigan worthy of the subject matter. A small admission is charged, which is put back into the museum project for maintenance, expansion and artifact acquisition. They also do exploration for shipwrecks throughout the Great Lakes and have been responsible for the discovery of many lost shipwrecks. The museum is seasonal.

When one first walks into the museum, they are met by a receptionist, who gives out a pamphlet that lists the exhibits and artifacts and then directs

making them useless. The ship is going down fast, and fates are doubtful as the life jacketed crew hit the water. Superior devours them. The last thing the captain sees is the flashing beacon of the Whitefish Point Lighthouse and prays that at least some of them can make it to the shore...but he knows that the lake shows no mercy for those that brave its waters.

Shipwrecks are a tragic fact and constant hazard of Lake Superior and all of the Great Lakes, but no other single place has been the site of more shipwrecks than the Whitefish Point waters between Grand Marais and Paradise, Michigan. The intense shipping traffic and narrowness of the strait, as the lake flows down you through a set of double doors. Inside is a shadowy dark room lined with displays of artifacts highlighted by spotlights. These spotlights are the only light source in the room, which gives a unique eerie effect. Then, one is met with the display of a carved wooden eagle encased in a glass cubicle. The eagle once adorned the pilot house of a steamer named *Vienna*. It is a striking sight, but immediately behind it is another attention grabber. Encased in glass is the bell from the legendary ship *Edmund Fitzgerald*. It was recovered from the ship several years ago and now is a centerpiece of the museum.

In the center of the room stands a massive brass and glass Fresnel lens. This particular device is for placement over the top of the source light that emanates from the lighthouse tower, creating its intense beam of light. This artifact is so big that the ceiling had to be specially cut to accommodate its height.

The entire museum's other exhibits line its walls. There are hundreds of different items representing many ships and incidents that occurred in the area. Also included are many photographs and newspaper clippings depicting the lives and deaths of each of the lighthouse's subjects. The subject matter is fascinating, educational and gripping. There are scale models of each ship that is profiled, including one of the *Edmund Fitzgerald*. The models' workmanship is excellent.

In a dark, far corner, there is a diorama: three divers, suspended from the ceiling, hang above a set of ribs – mounted on a wall - from the ship *Independence*. The life-size figures appear as if they are diving down to view the remains of the wreck. Because of the dark lighting, this gives a good impression of what wreck diving must be like. The display is life size, consequently taking up a good portion of a back corner.

The Edmund Fitzgerald ship's bell on display at Great Lakes Shipwreck Museum at Whitefish Point.

Then, when viewing is completed, one is directed to the lighthouse museum theater, where a documentary, describing the shipwreck history of the area and exploring the notoriety of the coast, plays. One section of the film is intense and riveting. It's footage of divers visiting the wrecks that lay on the bottom of the Great Lakes. The film is clear and well shot. It is worth the time it takes to stop in.

Situated behind the theater is a memorabilia and memento shop that has been set up inside a former storage shed. It has a nice atmosphere and stocks a good variety of items that are attractive and reasonable. Any profits from the store, of course, go back into the museum.

After viewing the museum, a walk on the sand and pebble beach is relaxing

This diver display of a wreck exploration is an exhibit that needs to be seen to believed at the Great Lakes Shipwreck Museum.

and nice. There are picnic tables here and a meal is fun, but supplies have to be purchased in Paradise. The lighthouse is also quite close to any of the Tahquamenon campgrounds, and this is a must see if you are staying there. While walking along the shore, one may appreciate the beauty of Lake Superior and reflect upon what its depth contains. Occasionally, carefully placed in the sand, there is a makeshift memorial to sailors who were victims of Lake Superior. The sight of the constant shipping - the sight of a freighter rounding the point - is continual and makes you wonder about fragile fates and the power of nature and particularly Lake Superior. The lazily rolling waves are so deceptive and harmless-looking.

The history of Lake Superior is unique, diverse and quite often tragic. The occasional tantrums that the lake throws can be costly in many ways and is a reality that influences life in the Upper Peninsula in every way. The Great Lakes Shipwreck Historical Society, with this museum, has put a large portion of that heritage on display and into perspective. The Society was formed in 1978 and is devoted to the recovery of shipwreck history. The Whitefish Point Lighthouse Shipwreck Museum is ample proof of those efforts. When visiting the Upper Peninsula, this should be on everyone's list.

About the Author

Mikel B. Classen has been writing about northern Michigan in newspapers and magazines for over 35 years, creating feature articles about the life and culture of Michigan's north country. He's written about travel, outdoors, the environment, Upper Peninsula history, and many other subjects. A journalist, historian, photographer, and author with a fascination about the world around him, he enjoys researching and writing about lost stories from the past. Currently, he is managing editor of the *U.P. Reader* and is a member of the board of directors for the Upper Peninsula Publishers and Authors Association.

Classen makes his home in the oldest city in Michigan, historic Sault Ste. Marie. He collects out-of-print history books and historical photographs and prints of Upper Michigan. At Northern Michigan University, he studied English, history, journalism, and photography. He lives with his wife, Mary L. Underwood, and his Labrador retriever, Gidget.

His book *Au Sable Point Lighthouse: Beacon on Lake Superior's Shipwreck Coast* was published in 2014, and his book *Teddy Roosevelt and the Marquette Libel Trial* was published in 2015. The History Press published both. He has a book of fiction called *Lake Superior Tales*, published by Modern History Press.

To learn more about Mikel B. Classen and to see more of his work, go to his website at www.mikelclassen.com.

Bibliography

Akogibing: A History of the Lake Gogebic Region with Emphasis on the Village of Bergland; Lulich, Marko; Marko Lulich, 1998

Alger County: A Centennial History; Symon, Charles A.; Bayshore Press, 1986

City of the Rapids: Sault Ste. Marie's Heritage; Arbic, Bernie; Priscilla Press, 2003

Dickenson County Michigan: From Earliest Times Through the Twenties; Cummings, William John; Dickenson County Board of Commissioners, 1991

Grand Island Story; Castle, Beatrice Hanscom; John M. Longyear Research Library, 1964

Great Lakes Crime; Stonehouse, Frederick; Avery Press, 2004

History of Iron County Michigan; Hill, Jack; Norway Current, 1976

History of the Ottawa and Chippewa Indians of Michigan; Blackbird, Andrew J.; Ypsilanti Job Printing, 1887

History of the Upper Peninsula of Michigan; author unknown; Western Historical Company, 1883

Honorable Peter White, The; Williams, Ralph D.; Penton Publishing, 1907

Incredible Seney; Reimann, Lewis C.; Avery Color Studios, 1982

Michigan Ghost Towns: Upper Peninsula Volume III; Dodge, Roy L.; Glendon Publishing, 1973

Old Fort Drummond: Drummond Island; Cook, Samuel F.; Robert Smith Printing 1896

Reflections from Old Crystal Falls; Hoffman, Bernie; Bernie Hoffman, 1995

Seney National Wildlife Refuge: It's Story; Losey, Elizabeth Browne; Lake Superior Press, 2003

Seul Choix Point: Gulliver Michigan; Fischer, Marilyn S.; Gulliver Historical Society, 2001

Superior Heartland; Rydholm, C. Fred; C. Fred Rydholm, 1990

This Ontonagon Country: Story of an American Frontier; Jamison, James K.; Ontonagon Herald Company, 1948

Victoria, Gem of Forest Hill; Johnson, Bruce H.; Society for Restoration of Old Victoria, 1993

Voyageur's Harbor; Carter, James L.; Pilot Press, 1977

Map Key for Points North Map of the U.P.

Map Key Number	Chapter Title
1	Au Sable Point Lighthouse – Alger County
2	Au Train Rising – Alger County
3	Big Knob State Forest Campground – Mackinac County
4	Big Two Hearted River – Luce County
5	Black River – Gogebic County
6	Brevort Lakes – Mackinac County
7	Canyon Falls Roadside Park – Baraga County
8	Cornish Pump and Mining Museum – Dickinson County
9	Donnelley Wilderness Tract – Marquette County
10	Drummond Island – Chippewa County
11	Eben Ice Caves – Alger County
12	Fortune Lakes, Bewabic Historical State Park – Iron County
13	Grand Island for a Grand Time – Alger County
14	Iron County Historical Museum – Iron County
15	Kingston Lake – Alger County.
16	Lake Antoine – Dickinson County
17	Lake Gogebic – Ontonagon County
18	Little Girls Point – Gogebic County
19	Little Presque Isle – Marquette County
20	Manistique Lakes and Curtis – Schoolcraft County
21	McCormick Wilderness Tract – Marquette County
22	McLain State Park – Houghton County
23	Monocle Lake – Chippewa County
24	North Country Trail – Entire UP
25	Old Victoria – Ontonagon County
26	Pentoga Park – Iron County
27	Pequaming: Ghost on the Water – Baraga County
28	Piers Gorge – Dickinson County
29	Porcupine Mountains – Ontonagon County
30	Portage Bay State Forest Campground – Delta County
31	Sault Ste. Marie Campgrounds – Chippewa County
32	Seney National Wildlife Refuge and Museum – Schoolcraft County
33	Seul Choix Pointe Lighthouse Park and Museum –Schoolcraft County
34	Museum of Ojibwa Culture – Mackinac County
35	Stonington Peninsula – Delta County
36	Sturgeon River Gorge Wilderness – Baraga County
37	Twin Lakes State Park – Houghton County
38	Tyoga Historical Pathway – Alger County
39	Woodland Park – Alger County
40	Whitefish Point Maritime Museum – Chippewa County

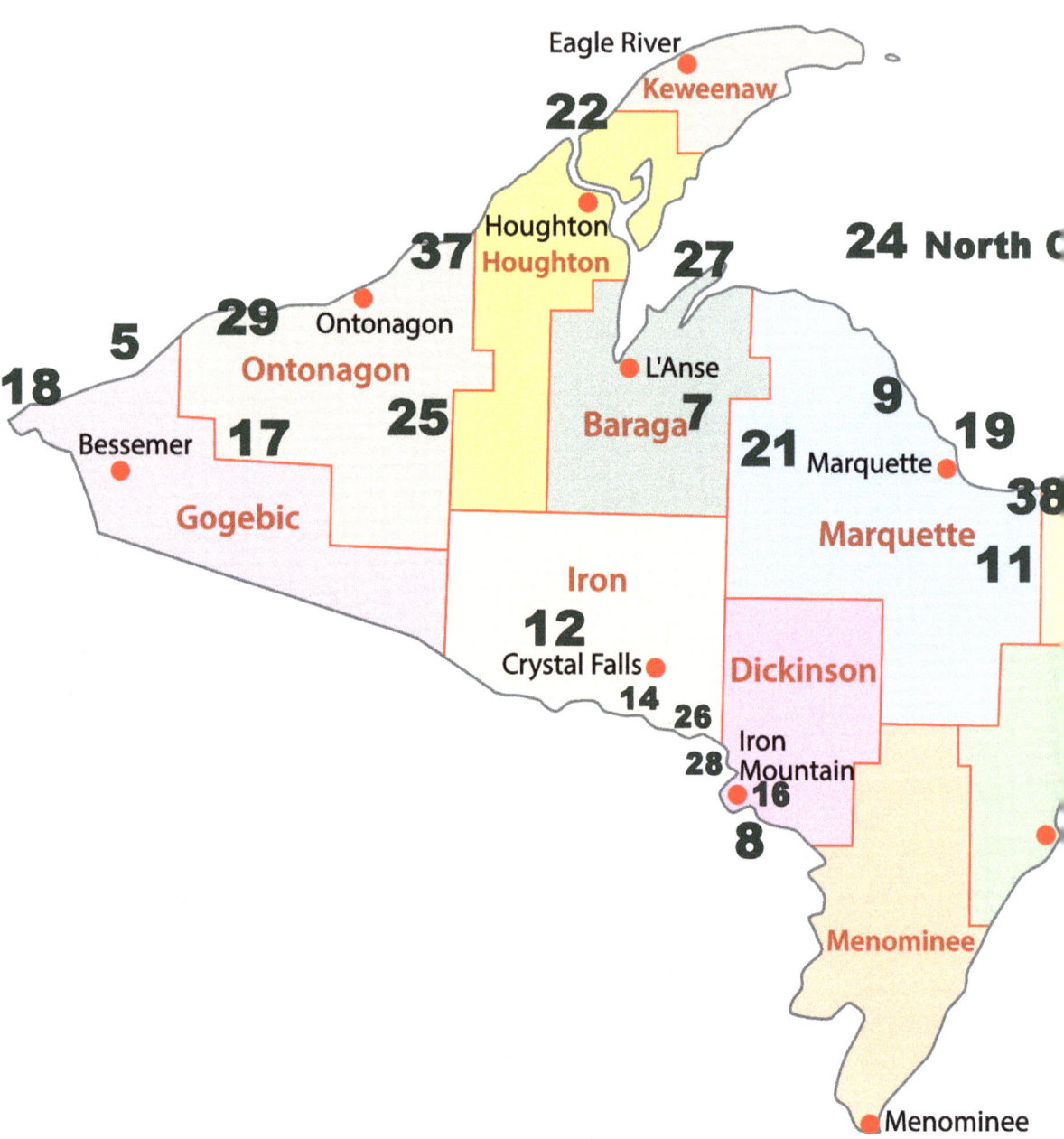

Eagle River

22 **Keweenaw**

Houghton
37 **Houghton**

29 Ontonagon **27**

5 **Ontonagon**

18 **25**

Bessemer **17** **Baraga** **7** L'Anse

Gogebic **21** Marquette **19**

24 North C

9

38

Marquette

11

Iron

12
Crystal Falls

Dickinson

14 **26**

28 Iron
Mountain

16

8

Menominee

Menominee

...try Trail (entire U.P.)

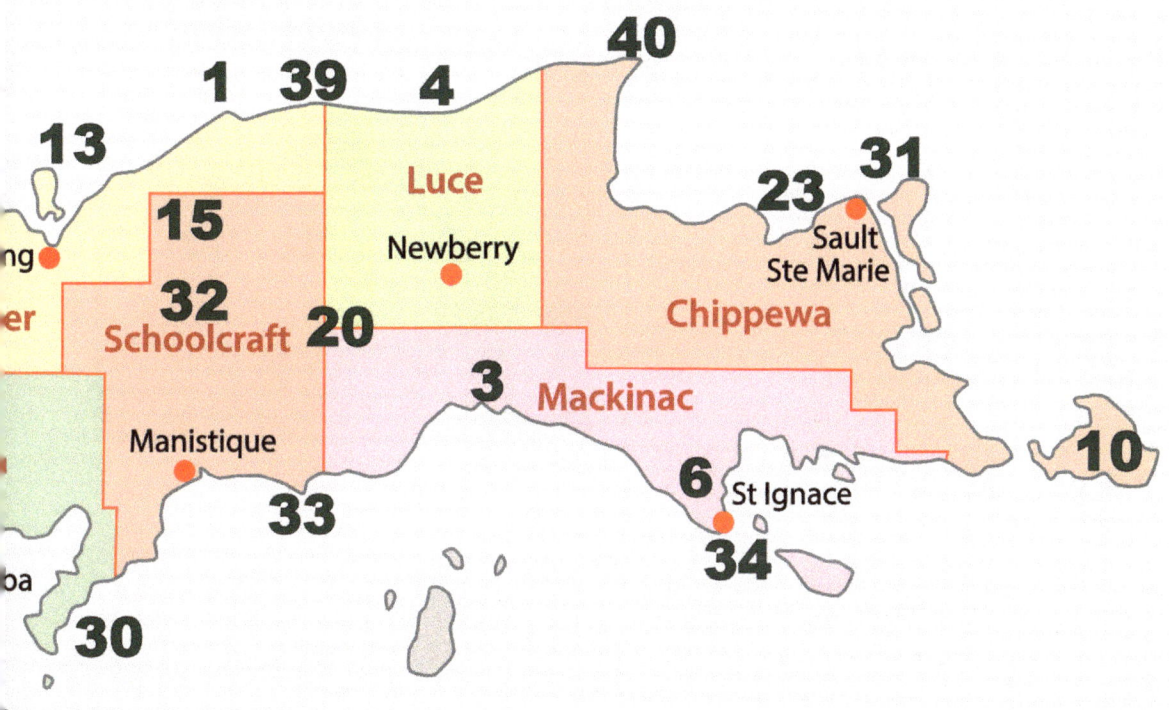

...ee map key on previous page to match numbers
...ith chapters in this book.

Join us for epic adventures in the U.P. on land and lakes!

Pirates, thieves, shipwrecks, sexy women, lost gold, and adventures on the Lake Superior frontier await you! In this book, you'll sail on a ship full of gold, outwit deadly shape-shifters, battle frontier outlaws and even meet the mysterious agent that Andrew Jackson called "the meanest man" he ever knew. Packed with action, adventure, humor, and suspense, this book has something for every reader. Journey to the wilds of the Lake Superior shoreline through ten stories that span the 19th century through present day including "The Wreck of the Marie Jenny," "The Bigg Man," "Wolf Killer," and "Bullets Shine Silver in the Moonlight."

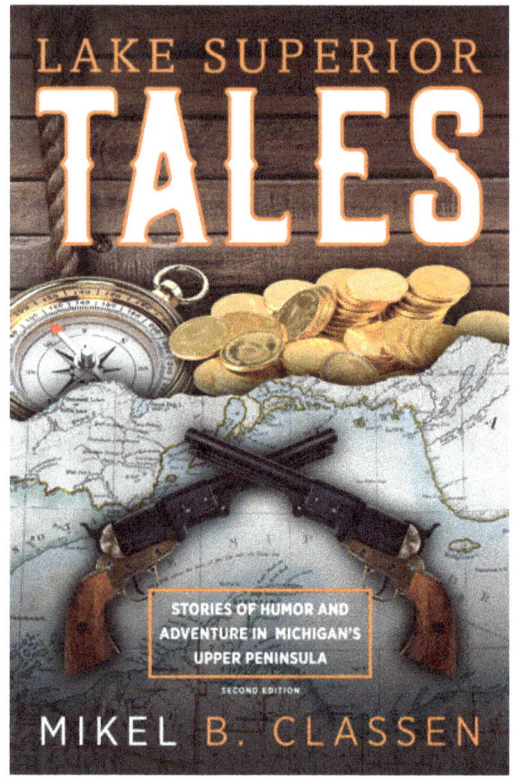

Mikel B. Classen is a longtime resident of Sault Sainte Marie in Michigan's Upper Peninsula. His intimacy of the region, the history and its culture gives this book a feel of authenticity that is rarely seen. As a writer, journalist, columnist, photographer, and editor with more than 30 years experience, his breadth of knowledge is unparalleled

"It's clear that Mikel B. Classen knows and loves the Lake Superior area of Michigan and brings it to life in a delightful way. If you want frequent laughs, unusual characters who jump off the page, and the fruit of a highly creative mind, you've got to read this little book."

-- Bob Rich, author, *Looking Through Water*

ISBN 978-1-61599-404-5

paperback * hardcover * eBook

From Modern History Press

Learn more at **www.MikelClassen.com**

U.P. Reader – Bringing Upper Michigan Literature to the World

Michigan's Upper Peninsula is blessed with a treasure trove of storytellers, poets, and historians, all seeking to capture a sense of Yooper Life from settler's days to the far-flung future. Since 2017, the *U.P. Reader* offers a rich collection of their voices that embraces the U.P.'s natural beauty and way of life, along with a few surprises.

These annual volumes take readers on U.P. road and boat trips from the Keweenaw to the Soo. Every page is rich with descriptions of the characters and culture that make the Upper Peninsula worth living in and writing about. U.P. writers span genres from humor to history and from science fiction to poetry. *U.P. Reader* also includes imaginative fiction from the Dandelion Cottage Short Story Award winners, honoring the amazing young writers enrolled in all of the U.P.'s schools. Featuring the words of some of the U.P.'s most prolific writers including Larry Buege, Mikel B. Classen, Deborah K. Frontiera, and Tyler R. Tichelaar.

"*U.P. Reader* offers a wonderful mix of storytelling, poetry, and Yooper culture. Here's to many future volumes!"

--Sonny Longtine, author of *Murder in Michigan's Upper Peninsula*

"As readers embark upon this storied landscape, they learn that the people of Michigan's Upper Peninsula offer a unique voice, a tribute to a timeless place too long silent."

--Sue Harrison, international bestselling author of *Mother Earth Father Sky*

The *U.P. Reader* is sponsored by the Upper Peninsula Publishers and Authors Association (UPPAA) a non-profit 501(c)3 corporation. A portion of proceeds from each copy sold will be donated to the UPPAA for its educational programming

paperback * hardcover * eBook

Learn more at **www.UPReader.org**

CPSIA information can be obtained
at www.ICGtesting.com
Printed in the USA
LVHW012116211220
674733LV00004B/32